# CANOEING

# THE BARNES SPORTS LIBRARY

**ARCHERY**
ARCHERY by Reichart and Keasey

**BADMINTON**
BETTER BADMINTON by Jackson and Swan

**BASEBALL**
HOW TO PITCH by Feller
BASEBALL by Jessee
THE DICTIONARY OF BASEBALL *With Official Rules* by Cummings
BASEBALL TECHNIQUES ILLUSTRATED by Allen and Micoleau

**BASKETBALL**
DRILLS AND FUNDAMENTALS by Bee
MAN-TO-MAN DEFENSE AND ATTACK by Bee
THE SCIENCE OF COACHING by Bee
ZONE DEFENSE AND ATTACK by Bee
BASKETBALL ILLUSTRATED by Hobson
BASKETBALL by Murphy
BASKETBALL FOR GIRLS by Meissner and Meyers
BASKETBALL TECHNIQUES ILLUSTRATED by Anderson and Micoleau

**BOWLING**
BOWLING FOR ALL by Falcaro and Goodman
BETTER BOWLING by Wilman
DUCK PIN BOWLING by Weinberg

**BOXING**
BOXING by Haislet

**CANOEING**
CANOEING by Handel

**CHEERLEADING**
CHEERLEADING AND MARCHING BANDS by Loken and Dypwick

**FENCING**
FENCING by Vince

**FISHING**
BLUEFISHING by Lyman
HOW TO TIE FLIES by Gregg
SURF FISHING by Evanoff
NATURAL FRESH WATER FISHING BAITS by Evanoff
FRESH AND SALT WATER SPINNING by Burns
FLY-ROD CASTING by Leonard
BAIT-ROD CASTING by Leonard
FISHING FOR WOMEN by Burns
NATURAL SALT WATER FISHING BAITS by Evanoff

**FOOTBALL**
FOOTBALL by Killinger
SIX-MAN FOOTBALL (Revised) by Duncan
FOOTBALL TECHNIQUES ILLUSTRATED by Moore and Micoleau

**GOLF**
GOLF ILLUSTRATED by Berg and Cox

**HOCKEY**
ICE HOCKEY by Jeremiah

**HUNTING**
DEER HUNTING by Park

**JIU-JITSU**
JIU-JITSU by Lowell

**KITES**
KITES by Fowler

**PHYSICAL CONDITIONING**
PHYSICAL CONDITIONING by Stafford and Duncan
WEIGHT LIFTING by Murray

**RIDING**
RIDING SIMPLIFIED by Self

**ROPING**
ROPING by Mason

**SELF DEFENSE**
SELF DEFENSE by Brown

**SKIING**
SKIING (Revised) by Prager

**SOFTBALL**
SOFTBALL by Noren
SOFTBALL FOR GIRLS (Revised) by Mitchell

**SWIMMING**
SWIMMING by Kiphuth

**TENNIS**
TENNIS by Jacobs
TENNIS MADE EASY by Budge
TENNIS TECHNIQUES ILLUSTRATED by Mace and Micoleau
TABLE TENNIS ILLUSTRATED by Cartland

**TRACK AND FIELD**
TRACK AND FIELD by Conger
TRACK TECHNIQUES ILLUSTRATED by Canham and Micoleau
FIELD TECHNIQUES ILLUSTRATED by Canham and Micoleau
CROSS-COUNTRY TECHNIQUES ILLUSTRATED by Canham and Micoleau

**VOLLEY BALL**
VOLLEY BALL by Laveaga

**WOODSMANSHIP**
WOODSMANSHIP by Mason

**WRESTLING**
WRESTING (Revised) by Gallagher and Peery

This library of sports books covers fundamentals, techniques, coaching and playing hints and equipment. Leading coaches and players have written these volumes. Photographs and drawings illustrate techniques, equipment and play.

# CANOEING

by

## Carle W. Handel

A. S. BARNES & COMPANY  NEW YORK

# Contents

# Introduction

Here is an unusual manual that combines the romance of wilderness places with technical skills; it is packed with clear-cut understandable instructions backed by reasonable explanations.

"The canoe is one of the safest crafts afloat" . . . "Its use is for all" . . . "Almost anyone can become efficient in its use" . . . these statements are given eloquent support.

Carle Handel has generously given of his experience that has been drawn from personal association with many expert guides on the canoe trails. In this book he portrays a canoe in a most interesting manner. It not only becomes a part of you, but you and the canoe become a part of the environment which ranges all the way from bayside in a resort town to dangerous churning rapids in the lone wilderness of the north country. You are introduced to the mysteries of woodslore, how the minnows indicate the channel of the river, the interpretive meaningful messages to be read in the clouds, the smoke from your campfire, the notch in the skyline, and the winds in the treetops.

Some of the more colorful definitions are "The difference between slow water and fast water is that in fast water you have less time to think." "An old timer on the river is one who has learned to portage around dangerous rapids rather than 'shoot' them." "Canoeing is different from any other type of water travel because part of the time you travel *under* your boat." (meaning portaging)

Here is one of the finest guides to canoeing that we know and, in the words of Winnabashoo, it will "whisper to you of faraway places," as well as to give you basic knowledge about the proper use, care and repair of a craft that is truly an American heritage.

Wes H. Klusmann
*National Director of Camping*
*Boy Scouts of America*

## chapter 1

# The Canoe, an American Heritage

"The aborigines of this new continent have long slender boats made of bark of the birchen trees. They move with speed propelled by paddles, even when heavily laden, and are carried around obstacles with surprising ease. It is said that large groups of the natives travel great distances over routes known only to them." So stated Jacques Cartier, an early explorer in the sixteenth century.

The mention of the canoe always conjures up the picture of the early days of our history, of the Indian, the pioneer, the explorer, the French *coureur de bois* and the Hudson's Bay Company brigades. It stands for adventure into quiet waters or roaring rapids, into the ancient ways of the rivers and lakes. It revives primitive instincts of exploration and the call to hunt, fish and camp. It is a challenge to skill, to the physical ability to take the long trail into new country. Few other sports combine such skills with the beauty of rivers, lakes or lagoons. And no other sport gives the same quiet peace of mind to those who seek rest from noisy overcrowded civilization, with its nerve-straining tensions and softening influences.

Nor does one have to seek for wilderness trails alone. To canoe down the back-yard way on a stream winding through pastoral land can be a surprisingly satisfying experience, filled with small adventures. For the nature student or lover of the out of doors, canoeing is a revelation, opening a whole new view of the animal, bird, insect, fish and plant life of our country.

Nor is the canoe only for a few hardy adventurers or wealthy sportsmen. It is a poor man's as well as a rich man's sport. You can build your own canoe and paddles, or buy a fine craft with a small outlay of money. The canoe costs approximately the price of two good bicycles, and with care it will last for many years. It can be carried easily on your back to the nearest water, or can be hauled any distance on the top of an automobile. With proper handling and care, the upkeep and repair is small and inexpensive and can be done by you or your own people.

The great advantage of the canoe is that it goes with ease on waters impossible to travel with any other kind of watercraft. It can be lifted and carried around obstacles that would be impassable for any other boat. A second advantage is that the canoe takes a minimum of effort to navigate, and in energy-distance factors it is highly efficient, as observed by some of our earliest explorers. It was a major factor, with the long rifle and the tomahawk, in opening up the farthest early frontiers of our continent.

Here, at the beginning, let us clear up two misconceptions persistently held by many people. First, the canoe is one of the safest crafts afloat; second, its use is for all, as almost anyone can become efficient in handling the canoe. Nor is it a man's sport alone. Some of the finest canoeists I have known have been women, often weighing hardly one hundred pounds. They frequently become more proficient than men in handling a canoe and quickly learn that skill is superior to "bull strength." As soon as a youngster can lift one end of a canoe, he or she may be taught the fundamentals of paddling and handling it.

As to the canoe's safety, almost any storm can be ridden out if you keep your gravity low in the canoe. The childish idea that upsetting a canoe is routine is far from the truth. To the thousands of people who use them each day, and who travel thousands of miles every year in the canoe country, upsetting a canoe is practically unknown. In fact, most of the people in the canoe country can't even swim. On the rare occasion when an upset does occur, they need only to hang on to the canoe, which makes a good life preserver since it will float even when full of water.

This book is intended to open up a new world for the beginner and to be a handbook for old-timers. It will take you through the various steps of selecting your canoe, handling and paddling it, and negotiating lakes and rivers. It will discuss packing, poling, portaging, canoe repair and care, canoe safety, and other simple techniques of this great American sport. This text will be brief and specific and will stick to fundamentals. We hope that it will lead you to a most satisfying experience. We also hope this book will be your companion on many delightful trips.

*chapter 2*

# Canoe Parts

## History and Terminology

Most of the names of the parts of the canoe derive from sea tradition, undoubtedly originating with our early explorers, who were familiar with sailing ships. When they sent parties inland they hired Indians with canoes, which latter naturally inherited the terminology of the sailing ships.

Consequently, the front of a canoe is today called the "bow" (pronounced to rhyme with "cow"), and the rear end of the canoe is called the "stern." The right side is "starboard" and the left side "port." To go to the front of a canoe is to go "forward" and to go to the stern is to go "aft."

## Principles of Shape and Construction

One of the secrets of the strength, lightness and efficiency of the canoe is the use of the curve or bow construction, which gives a maximum degree of rigidity and bracing strength. Almost every part of a canoe is built in a curve, the bending of which gives curved tension, increasing the strength per pound and thus eliminating the need of heavy shoring and bracing. The curved streamlining of a canoe also gives it maximum efficiency in passing through the water. The bow construction makes it highly maneuverable, thereby adding to the value and safety of the craft. The canoe draws a minimum depth of water and can therefore pass through shallows even with a heavy load, making it an ideal craft for a wide variety of sport and travel, especially along the streams of a wild country.

## The Gunwales or Gunnels

Looking down into a canoe, one sees along each side from bow to stern two long curved strips of wood. The one on the outside is called the outwale and the one on the inside is called the

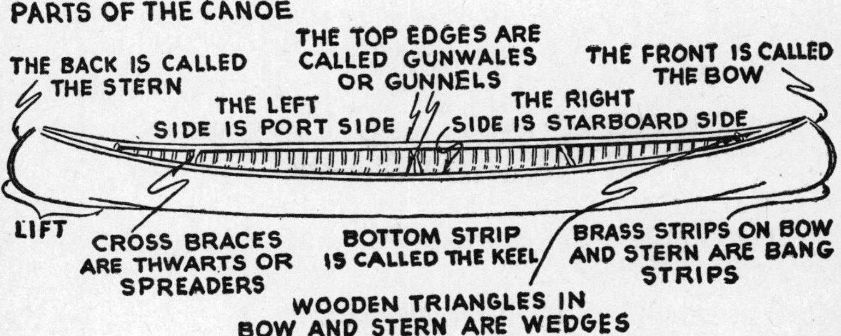



inwale; the two together are called the gunwale or gunnel. Sailing ships had similar construction and since the gunnel was one of the strongest parts of a ship, cannon platforms were arranged along it and could stand the shock of firing. The canoe inherited this term from the gun row on the heavy beam of a ship.

## The Ribs

Between the inwale and the outwale one finds the ends of curved strips at right angles to the gunnels, bent down across the bottom and fastened between the opposite gunnel. These strips are strong, usually made of spruce, sometimes cypress, and are known as the ribs. They give strength and rigidity to the canoe, making it strong from both inside and outside pressures.

## The Planking

Over the outside of the ribs of the canoe is a covering of thin cedar boards known as planking, which gives a smooth surface on which the canvas can be stretched. The planking should be tight, with no cracks or holes of any kind, so that sand cannot work in between it and the canvas to form a sand bubble and cause a leak. The planking and ribs are covered with several coats of waterproof varnish on the inside; on the outside the planking is usually heavily treated with linseed oil before the canvas is stretched over it.

### The Covering

Over the outside of the planking the canvas is stretched, carefully fitted, cut to shape. Then the ends are carefully sewn. It is a real art to stretch canvas properly on a canoe. Once it is tight and smooth, all holes at the point of sewing are painted with linseed oil and filled with white lead. Then the entire canvas is heavily painted with linseed oil and allowed to dry. This is followed by several coats of white lead-base paint of color desired and topped with two good coats of Spar varnish, inside and out.

When buying a canoe be sure its canvas is good weight of duck. The life of your canoe and the value of your purchase depends on the use of good canvas of medium weight, filled and painted with good paint. Watch out for blisters and cracks, and give especial attention to the tucking at the ends, as a great deal depends on proper covering and waterproofing.

### The Keel

This is the strip of wood that runs along the bottom from the bow to the stern on the outside of the canoe. It is used to protect the bottom of the canoe from coming in contact with any object

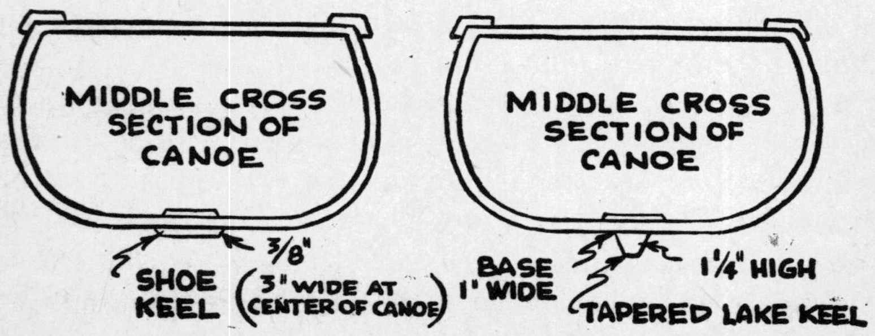

either in the water or out. (In a sailboat it is used as the centerboard to prevent sideslipping by wind in open water.)

There are two types of keel; the lake-keel which is about an inch high and an inch wide at the base, and the shoe-keel which is two to three inches wide and only about a quarter of an inch thick. The lake-keel is good for lake paddling, but the shoe-keel is best for river paddling as sideslipping the canoe is part of maneuvering up and downstream. In buying a canoe, remember that the shoe-keel is the best all-around keel. It may have more wind-slip in the lakes, but it is more maneuverable and therefore desirable in river navigation. Be sure that the screws that hold the keel to the canoe are of solid brass, not coated. In fact, be sure that all hardware on your canoe is of brass, as steel will rust, especially in salt water.

### The Bang Strip

Around the outside of the curved end of both the bow and the stern is a brass metal strip usually half round, which is called the bang strip, or sometimes, the fender. These are very important as they protect the delicate front edge of the canoe from impact, abrasion or breaking. They shield the stitched ends of the canvas from rocks, logs and brush. They must be tightly fastened with brass screws and extend full length from the decking to the keel. When buying a canoe or when surveying a canoe for repair, be sure that the strips are tight. Occasionally go over the screws of your canoe with a screw driver to be sure that they haven't worked loose. Never hit the bang strip with a hammer as it tends to loosen the entire strip.

### The Lift and Tumble Home

When selecting a canoe be sure that at the bottom of the bow and stern there are lifts of a couple of inches that reach about two feet along the bottom. This gives an upward lift when approaching waves in lakes or white water in rapids. Without the lift the boat would plow directly through, shipping water over the front. The lift also is of advantage when steering. Otherwise, if too low in the water, the sharp bow would act as a keel and make the canoe less maneuverable.

Directly in front of the bow-paddling position is a swelling out of the front of the canoe. A similar swelling can be observed in the stern. This is sometimes called the bulge or the tumble home. It should not be too tapering or too abrupt, as its function is to create displacement and raise the front weight after the bow has split a wave or white water. If it is not bulged out enough, like a snow plow, water will be shipped into the bow paddler's lap, while if it is too blunt, it will impede forward progress. If too narrow, it will uncomfortably crowd the bow paddler who is down on his knees.

### The Spreaders or Thwarts

The gunwales are held apart by the thwarts or spreaders. These brace the canoe, act as seats or rests for the paddlers, and serve as a carrying beam when the canoe is carried or portaged. Inspect the spreaders to be sure that they are straight-grained hardwood such as ash or hickory. Maple and birch are not as good because they have a tendency to warp and crack. The ends must be bolted on both top and bottom with plates or washers. Of course, these must be made of brass to prevent rusting.

It is important that the thwarts be placed so that the paddlers are in good fore and aft positions to balance the canoe without too much side reach. To allow space for the bow paddler, the front thwart is farther from the front end than the stern thwart is from the rear end. The center thwart must be on the balance of the canoe if you are going to do any portaging. When buying a canoe, give careful attention to these important points.

### The Seats

Seats are not necessary in a canoe but many people prefer to have them. They should have caned bottoms and should not be too far below the gunnels so that when you are on your knees paddling your feet can go back under them with plenty of room. In case of an emergency or upset you want plenty of room so that you can extricate your feet quickly without getting them caught. This is an important safety factor.

### The Wedges or Decking

In both the bow and the stern, where the gunnels meet, there is a wedge-shaped piece of wood that acts as an end brace. If these come back more than ten inches, they are called decking. Otherwise they are called wedges. They round up in the middle, and besides being a brace, they shed any spray or water that comes over. There is often a raised ridge to gutter the water off each side.

### The Rope, Ring, Hole or Cleat

Every canoe should have an arrangement for fastening a rope on both the bow and the stern wedges. This usually consists of a ring (welded) for rope attachment, but sometimes it is a hole in the deck or a cleat through which to fasten a line to tie up or pull the canoe.

### The Bow and Stern Shape

Attention should also be given to the height of the bow and stern. The best example of proper height is exhibited in the low-prowed guide-model canoe. If your bow and stern rise too high they weather-vane in the wind, which adds to the difficulty of steering and also makes the canoe hard to store, carry or turn over. Purchase a canoe with a low prow. The high-prowed birchbark of the Indian is artistic and fancy and seen only in the movies or in the drawings of artists who never saw a real birchbark or elmbark canoe. I have seen hundreds of them and have traveled hundreds of miles in a birchbark canoe, but I have never seen the high prows of art and movies. Even the largest freight canoes have the lines of the low-prowed guide-model canoe.

### Length, Width, Depth and Weight

The average two-man canoe is sixteen feet in length, with fourteen to sixteen inches draft or depth at the center thwart. As to weight, here is a word of caution. Many salesmen will emphasize the lightness of a canoe. Look for quality first. Be sure that the material is strong and the craft well finished. To sacrifice quality just to save weight is foolhardy and usually means that the manufacturer is saving money at your expense by cutting down on materials. I would rather have a few pounds extra than a leaky canoe, broken ribs or planking, or a broken thwart. A sixteen-foot canoe, new and dry, usually weighs from seventy to eighty pounds. A word should be said concerning long trips and heavy loads. A seventeen-foot canoe is better for heavy loads, white water and waves. It will be about twenty-five pounds heavier than a sixteen-foot canoe and a little harder to paddle, but you gain a great deal in stability and comfort.

As a final caution, know your canoe parts and their correct names. When you buy a canoe, look carefully at each detail mentioned above. It will help you to get the best for your money.

In remote regions of some canoe countries people use local names for certain canoe parts. Who are we to say they are wrong? Please, in the interest of harmony, don't correct them or argue with them. Maybe their terminology is as correct as yours. It's a matter of viewpoint.

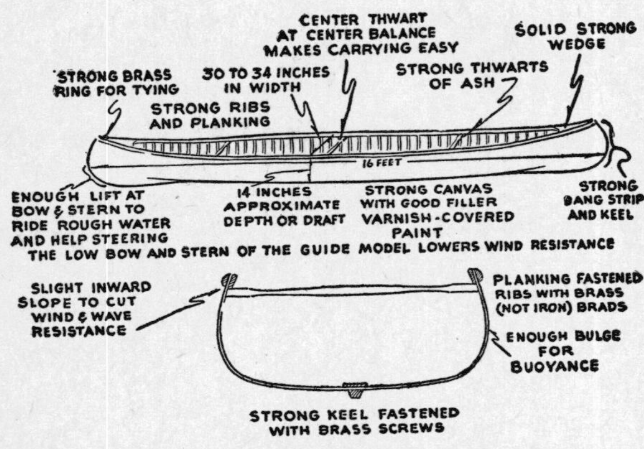


## The Paddles

Now that you know how to select and buy a canoe, let's look at paddles. The paddle is second in importance only to the canoe. When you are paddling all day on a canoe trip, you will beat about twenty-five to thirty strokes a minute, about four hundred and fifty to the mile, and about one thousand strokes per continuous hour. In a good long day you will beat between fifteen thousand and eighteen thousand strokes or an approximate equivalent of fifty-four thousand foot-pounds of work. That is about the same amount of energy that it takes to shovel coal on a steam passenger train for a three hundred and fifty mile run. On this basis, such small matters as weight, balance, varnish, spring, shape and grip become very important. The best paddles are made of spruce, al-

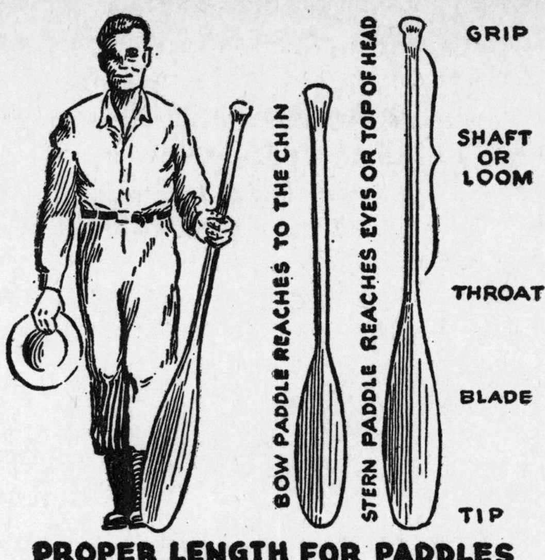



**PROPER LENGTH FOR PADDLES**

though some people prefer maple or ash. Spruce is lighter, does not warp and crack like maple and does not split like ash.

The paddle should be smooth, with a good comfortable grip, straight-grained, and well oiled or thoroughly varnished.

As to size, the bow paddle, when stood on end, should reach to the bow paddler's chin. The stern paddle should, when stood on end, reach to the stern paddler's eyes or even to the top of his head. The extra length of the stern paddle is necessary for added leverage in steering.

The names of the various parts of the paddle from top to bottom are the grip, the shaft or loom, the throat, the blade and the tip. For their positions, see the accompanying drawing. The various shapes of blades and grips and their names may be seen in the same drawing.

The width and length of the blade is important. If your blade is too big, you will soon tire. If it is too small, you waste energy and have less control of your canoe. The blade should be at least a third of the length of the paddle and should be about six inches wide at the widest part. Of course, for children, smaller paddles are used.

The spring of a paddle is important because it acts as a shock absorber, adding to the leverage, and thus to the more efficient progress of the canoe. In this respect, the maple paddle is superior to the spruce or ash paddles which have a tendency to be a little stiff. However, I prefer the spruce paddle because of its lightness.

Select your paddles carefully and fit them to your own size and needs. Remember that an extra paddle should be carried on long trips. Of course, in a real emergency, using a good axe and a knife, you can make a paddle in an hour. The Indians did it regularly. Why shouldn't you?

## chapter 3

# Handling and Carrying the Canoe

Before you ever dip a paddle into the water, it is essential to learn to use great care in handling the canoe on land. It is very important to practice carrying the canoe, shipping it, launching or landing it and also beaching and storing it. Over ninety per cent of the breaking and injuring of canoes is done on land. Once we watched a man, whom we had just hired as guide, buy a beautiful new canoe at an outfitter's. To our horror, the clerk, after stripping the burlap packing off, climbed inside with a putty knife to scrape off some paper stuck to the thin planking. After we told him, in picturesque language, never to climb into a canoe on land and above all not to gouge the thin planking, that the first rain would soak off the paper, he started to drag the canoe along the floor. More picturesque language following, and when we insisted that the canoe be carried, the clerk grabbed it up by the middle and whirled it around. He did not see an anvil fastened to a large block of wood, and the point of the anvil crashed through the beautifully painted bow of the new canoe. The outfitter told us that it was the third canoe the clerk had broken during the year and I suggested that perhaps the clerk should confine his activities to moving anvils. We had to scurry around and rent a canoe, at extra cost, and almost missed getting it and our duffel aboard the train that was to take us two hundred and fifty miles up into the "bush country."

A canoe is a light craft and can be picked up easily if one knows the balance points of good leverage.

*One-Man Lifts and Carries*

When you are picking up a canoe alone you should use the carry to fit the distance. If it is not more than fifty feet, carry the canoe on your hip. If it is a hundred yards or so, roll it up, turning

the bottom up with you underneath, resting the center thwart on your shoulders. However, if the distance is longer, tie your paddles into a paddle yoke for a more comfortable carry. To learn to fix a paddle yoke, see illustration.

Before you pick up a canoe, look around and locate any hazards underfoot and in the air, such as branches, stubs, roots or sharp rocks. Many a trip has been spoiled by a sprained back or a hole in the canoe because this was not done. If the canoe is lying bottom side up, carefully roll it over, top side up. Then stand at the center thwart at the center of balance facing the canoe. Reach down with both hands and turn the canoe upon its side until it lies with the bottom resting on your knees. This is the basic position for all one-man pickups. Then, holding the near gunnel with the left hand, bend and reach as far over on the center thwart as possible with the right hand. Get the canoe bottom up tight on the knees. Then as you give an upward pull with your right hand across the thwart, drop your hips and bend your knees slightly. The canoe should roll into your lap. Kick up with your toes as the canoe rolls upward. Then twist the body toward the front of the canoe or clockwise as you straighten up; keep the right hand coming on over the head, until the thwart rests on the shoulders.

To put the canoe down, reverse the process. Put your hands on the gunnels, push up and twist the body counterclockwise with the right hand holding the center thwart at the right ground, the left hand holding the left gunnel. The canoe is then rolled down to the bent knees and is eased to the ground. Always, before putting down a canoe, look around for obstructions on the ground and in the air that might scratch or puncture the canoe or interfere with your drop.

For short carries of a few yards for one man, the canoe can be rolled up on the hip and carried by holding the center thwart.

### Two-Man Lifts and Carries

The two-man lift is exactly like the one-man lift except that the men stand on the same side opposite the front and rear thwarts or seats. With the left hand on the near gunnel, they roll the canoe on its side, then reach across to the opposite gunnel, with the right hand, roll the canoe up overhead with the stern thwart or seat resting on the shoulders of the sternman and the front seat or thwart resting on the shoulders of the bowman. For short carries of a few yards, the canoe can be carried by men standing opposite the center thwart and hooking the fingers under the inwale. They can lift together and carry forward or backward as the need may be. For longer carries, say twenty-five yards, grasp the front or back wedges and lift while walking forward. Do not roll up the canoe and try to carry with the wedges resting on the shoulder.

Canoes can sometimes be broken this way if one stumbles or slips. If the canoe is to be carried bottom up, get underneath, for one man braces and steadies the other in case of an accident.

### Loading and Shipping a Canoe

In case you are going to load your canoe in a freight car, a baggage car or a large truck, load carefully, then tie the canoe up overhead with rope slings fore and aft. Put padding under the ropes, as jostling will work the paint off or crack the planking or ribs. If you are loading on an automobile top, have a luggage carrier and pad and tie down tight. If the canoe hangs out over the end, red flag it. Or, if you drive through brush or overhead branches, be careful. Bad scratches or breaks may occur. Also, if the canoe is on top of the car park in the shade as hot sun often checks or blisters the varnish or paint.

Under no circumstances allow duffel or other heavy material to be placed in the canoe during shipping. This can break or wear holes very quickly. In airplane transport, tie the canoe very tight with the top sides up toward the belly of the plane, so the shape of the canoe will streamline into the air stream, as air vibration is great at one hundred miles per hour or more. Not only the canoe, but the plane as well, can be wrecked if the canoe is not tied tightly. Carrying a canoe above the pontoons of an airplane is risky business any way you look at it.

### One-Man Launching and Docking

As soon as the pickups and carries are mastered, practice launching and docking your canoe.

When launching a canoe alone, roll the canoe up on your knees, holding to the gunnel with both hands. After the canoe is safe, step sideways toward the water until the bow starts into the water. Then, standing at the water's edge, walk your hands along the canoe, sliding it full length into the water. Resting the tip of the stern on the beach, secure the rope tied to the ring as a precaution against wind or current, which might carry your canoe away in the twinkling of an eye. I once knew of a man marooned on an island for several days before he was fortunately picked up, because the wind blew his canoe away.

In beaching or docking, use reverse procedure to land the canoe. Grasp the gunnel and hand-walk the canoe shoreward until the center balance is reached. Roll the canoe up on your knees and walk sideways to where you want to put the canoe down.

### Two-Man Launching and Docking

The same procedure is used in a two-man launching except that the men stand opposite the middle lift and hand-walk the canoe into or out of the water.

### Laying up the Canoe on Shore

Canoe racks are fine for shore storage, but on the trail the canoes are laid on the ground. Always carry the canoes well back from the water's edge. Then roll them over, bottom side up, with the bottom facing the open water so that a sudden storm or gust of wind will not blow them over or break them. In case you are going to leave for several days, carry the canoes well inshore, under the small trees if possible; then tie them down. Clean any fish or grease off them and scrub them thoroughly so porcupines won't gnaw on them. Some guides rub kerosene on the seats and spreader to discourage both bears and porcupines. Do not put canoes under large trees or you may find a limb through your canoe when you return.

### One-Man Loading or Unloading

When loading a one-man canoe always have your rope, line or painter, as it is variously called, tied up. If the water is deep enough, carefully run your canoe parallel with and adjacent to the shore. Then distribute the load so that the paddler will balance up the canoe once aboard. If the load is light, put it in the stern and tie in tightly. Then paddle facing the stern, resting against the bow thwart. If without a load, the paddler gets down on his knees and rests against the center thwart. Otherwise the canoe will wind-vane and be unstable, poorly balanced and hard to control.

In docking, one man can come carefully up on a sandy beach, or come in sideways, picking a rock or log on which to land. Once at the dock or beach, you get ashore in the following fashion. Holding the paddle in your hands, lay it across the gunnels, with your fingers reaching around the paddle and holding the gunnels. Rise from your knees, keeping the weight on your hands. Keep your feet in the center line of the canoe, toe in and balanced, keeping your head down, and put your foot ashore. Get a good footing, shove up arms, shift weight to leg on shore and then with one motion, step ashore. Be sure to keep a paddle in your hand with which to reach for the canoe. It is also a good idea to hold the tether line in your hand as you land.

### Two-Man Loading and Unloading

After the canoe is eased into the water, bow first, you are ready to load. A word of caution: do not carry sharp-edged boxes or other material. If you have to transport any sharp-edged equipment, see that it is padded, or you may find a hole in the bottom of your canoe.

When the stern is resting on the edge of the shore, all equipment is stacked within easy reach of the canoe. The sternman holds the end of the canoe tightly between his legs to steady it while the bowman backs into the canoe, keeping low and center. Then the sternman, still holding the canoe steady between his legs, passes the duffel up to the bowman who stows it so that it balances up the canoe, covering it with a tarpaulin and tying it in securely. All duffel should be tied in at all times. If waves, rain or white water are anticipated, lay poles in the bottom to keep the bottom of the duffel from getting wet. Perishable material such as food, cameras or first-aid kits should always be put in the packs on top to protect them from dampness.

*Getting Underway*

Once the canoe is loaded, the duffel covered and tied down, the bowman gets down on his knees, puts his paddle in the water to steady the craft, and then orders the sternman to be ready to shove off. The sternman slides the canoe into the water, keeping his weight on shore until the last minute. He lays his paddle across the gunnel, holding it and the gunnel with both hands. Then, head down, placing one foot in the center of the canoe, he shifts his weight to the canoe and shoves off with a foot on shore. While still holding his hands on the gunnel, he brings the other foot into the canoe, drops to his knees and gets his paddle into the water. Then they are underway.

In landing, the process is just the reverse. The bowman lands, taking his paddle with him, and holds the canoe between his knees while the sternman unties and passes up the duffel to him. The bowman holds the canoe between his knees until the sternman is ashore. Then, together, they carry the canoe on shore as previously described. It is then laid up or prepared for the portage as the need may be.

As we go on in this book you will see that good canoemanship is teamwork between the bowman and the sternman.

It might also be observed that in the canoe country a man is judged largely on his launching or landing of a canoe by the rule: no scratches on the bottom and no water on his feet. A good canoeman seldom steps in the water, either in launching or landing, except in a rare emergency. It is a good code to practice, especially if you are going into the canoe country.

*chapter 4*

# Paddling the Canoe

The principles of handling and paddling a canoe are simple, and once they are understood, almost anyone can become proficient with practice. I have no patience with so-called experts who feed their egos by posing as the possessors of superior knowledge, and who confuse people with a screen of technical language. I was once present at a gathering at Bear Island Hudson's Bay Post where a group of people had asked to be initiated into the mysteries of canoeing. The self-appointed instructor, who had a few degrees and who taught on the faculty of a large university, started out by saying that he had special knowledge derived from living with the Indians. Actually, his knowledge of Indians was one short trip with Joe Friday, an Ojibway guide. Joe was doing his duty as a guide and had taught him the fundamentals of paddling a canoe. From his heights, the instructor had a self-indulgent pity for these poor ignorant masses. He put on a very mediocre demonstration, using technical language, then advised that, since the canoe was a craft requiring great skill, they had better venture out only as baggage with a guide or himself to do the paddling.

29

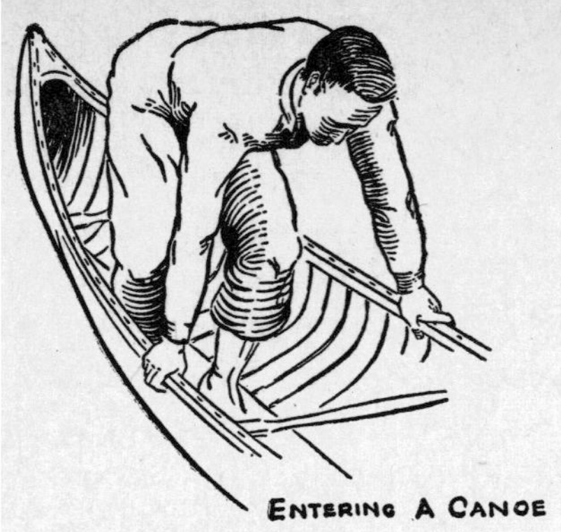



Tom Marsh, a Canadian and an excellent bushman, and I listened quietly (we had just finished a long trip through the back country covering fifteen hundred miles). Finally, the instructor superficially asked if there were any questions. Marsh, in his quiet polite English way, asked one or two questions and received vague and irritated answers. Finally Marsh said to the twenty-five or thirty people there that he would teach them all to paddle and handle a canoe in an hour. Tom and I soon had both men and women launching canoes, getting into them properly, paddling in a straight line, making right and left, long and short turns, using jam or stopping strokes, landing and stacking their canoes. Everybody had a wonderful time, and returned home full of the joy of adventure into a new world, with respect for and confidence in the canoe. Needless to say, we received the undying hatred of the self-styled expert.

The canoe is a long streamlined craft usually propelled by two paddlers, one about four feet from the front tip of the canoe and one about two and a half feet from the back tip. The craft is propelled by paddles which are grasped in the hands of the paddlers. The paddle has a grip at the top to fit the hand and a round shaft or loom about an inch in diameter running two thirds of the length of the paddle. The lower third of the paddle is a flat streamlined blade, the end of which is called the tip; the place where the blade meets the round shaft is known as the throat. We will henceforth use the terms grip, shaft, throat, blade and tip to designate parts of the paddle from top to bottom.

There are several types of paddles, the selection of which has previously been discussed. (See illustration.) It is best that the bow and stern paddles be of the same type and shape as this gives better balance in paddling.

The principles of paddling are as follows: both paddlers, fore and aft, are down on their knees, resting their hips against the seat or thwart. If they could reach directly out in front of them and dip the blade at right angles at the center line of the canoe, pulling directly back between their knees, the canoe would go forward in a straight line, provided there was no wind or current. But this is not possible. They paddle on opposite sides and, by necessity, have

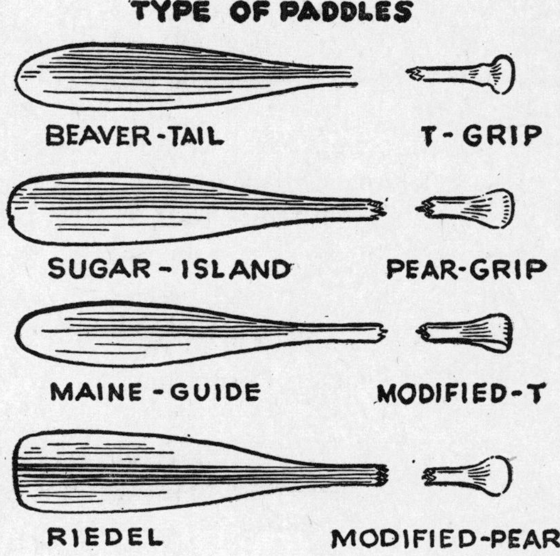


to reach out in the water and pull back. Stroking off the center line, as they do, tends to make the canoe turn away from the forward thrust created by the paddler pulling the paddle back. Therefore, steering is necessary in order to travel in a straight line in a canoe. Another factor causing imbalance is that the bow paddler is at a greater distance from the bow tip of the canoe than the stern paddler is from the stern tip. The last factor is that the directional pull of the bow paddler is toward the center of the canoe, cutting down his ability to steer. On the other hand, as the stern paddler pulls his paddle back, he moves toward the tapering end and center line of the canoe, giving more water area for steering. The fact that the sternman is nearer the tip of the canoe and in the slipstream of the water gives him the maximum advantage for steering. Consequently, the sternman, having at least a two-thirds steering advantage, is always in charge of the ship. He is captain, issuing the orders, and the bowman is first mate. The sternman's place in the canoe, by mechanical and steering necessity, makes it natural for him to be captain of the ship.

Let us get clearly in mind that most of the steering of the canoe is done at the stern, although the bow paddler does his share in places requiring turns and maneuvering. The sternman is in charge except in emergencies such as rapids, where the bowman acts automatically when split seconds mean avoiding disaster. The bowman, being in forward position, can usually see dangers, and it is his job to watch out for them. Often he doesn't have time to signal except by his actions, and the alert sternman follows through. Also, the sternman may be in charge of the craft, but the bowman sets the pace of the stroke. In other words, fine teamwork is a requirement for safety.

## Canoeing Strokes

There are three types of canoeing strokes:
1. Cruising strokes (going forward in a
                         straight line)
2. Draw or turning strokes (turning right
                                 or left)
3. Jam or stopping strokes (for quick stops,
                               for holding steady
                               as a keel, et cetera)

The first two are the better-known strokes and are used constantly in canoeing. However, the jam strokes are of vital importance when you need them.

## Cruising Strokes

By cruising strokes we mean those used to go forward in a straight line and keep the canoe on course. The mark of a tenderfoot is shown by changing sides. This is not only unnecessary and dangerous but also poor canoemanship. Once in the canoe, the sternman tells the bowman which side to paddle, and it is not necessary to change position all day.

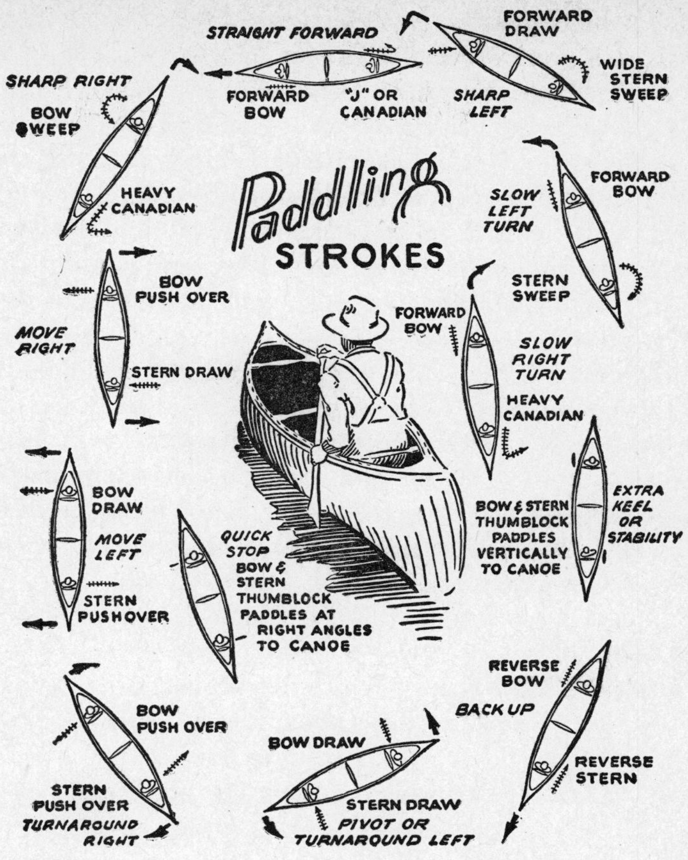


To begin with, the paddling position is important. Get a good comfortable pad under your knees, keeping your center of gravity low, and assume a relaxed position. Keep your back straight, head up, avoid sideswaying. The paddle is held by one hand at the top at the grip built for that purpose, while the other hand slides down the shaft to the throat of the paddle just above the blade. The top hand holds the grip firmly, while the lower hand is held loosely so that the paddle can be rotated in steering. The upper hand on the grip does the driving, with the elbow in close to the body. The drive of the upper hand is not just with the forearm but with the weight of the shoulder and body forming the forward power. On a canoe trip you are often driving a heavy load all day long. This is different from paddling an empty canoe around a lagoon in the city park. Consequently, you throw your weight against the paddle to develop efficient power with a minimum expenditure of energy. However, avoid swaying back and forth; rotate your body when necessary, but keep vertical. Use your shoulder muscles as much as possible. The lower hand acts as a fulcrum and the arm is always kept straight. Do not bend the elbow. Little if any power is created by the lower arm, although the sternman may use his lower arm for a small amount of power for guiding at the end of a stroke. The stroke is accomplished by swinging the lower arm forward until the paddle rests just out of the water, with the blade angling down and forward. With the upper arm close to the body and the hand directly in front of and close to the chin, you are ready for the stroke. Begin it by dipping the tip of the blade into the water. As soon as a good purchase is felt on the water, the upper arm and shoulder give the forward driving power while, as has been mentioned, the lower arm acts as a fulcrum.

The stroke is finished when it reaches the hip at your side pocket, the vertical bottom of the arc made by the paddle. Swing the paddle out of the water sideways, keeping the lower arm straight. Any further carrying back of the paddle in the arc is a waste of energy—in fact, a hindrance to the forward motion of the canoe, except for steering purposes by the sternman, who carries his stroke far enough beyond the hip to pull the front end of the canoe into line. The bow paddler always pulls his paddle out at the hip. With the lower arm straight, the paddle is pulled out, twisted flat or parallel to the water, and swung forward in a side arc into position for another stroke. Keeping the returning paddle parallel to the water is called feathering, and saves a great deal of energy as it cuts down the wind resistance to the forward motion of the paddle. This is important especially on a windy day. Pulling out at the hip and swinging the paddle gives the choppy swinging motion to paddling. You are executing a quarter-circle arc vertically, while rowing executes a half-circle arc horizontally. The principle of paddling is entirely different from rowing a boat. Paddling a canoe should not be taught at the same time with rowing a boat as it would be confusing.

Now let us see how to complete the cruising stroke, giving attention to the steering required by the stern paddler. The paddlers are in position. Together they dip their paddles and make the stroke in unison. The bowman swings his paddle out of the water at the hip, but the sternman carries on back, completing the vertical arc another eighth of a circle. As the blade passes his hip, the hand on the grip twists downward, making the paddle vertical in the water. Since the canoe has a tendency to swing away from the side of the stern paddler, he brings it back in line by swinging the paddle outward vertically, making a hook or "J." This is called the "hook" of the "J" stroke and is used as a cruising stroke only in the stern.

At this point another stroke should be recognized which is more efficient than the J or hook stroke. It is widely used in the "bush" country of Canada and is called the *Canadian stroke*. The paddle passes the hip of the sternman a few inches instead of being vertical and pushed outward as in the J stroke, and the outside edge is flipped forward, angling down slightly into the water so that the water spills up over the returning paddle as over a flat rock in a rapids. Then, because the blade has a tendency to plane downward in the water, it is pulled forward again, prying upward, thereby pulling the canoe back into line. As the blade is swung just a little forward of the hip, it is flipped out of the water and a new stroke begins. The main difference between the J and the Canadian stroke is that in the J stroke the paddle is in the water fifty per cent of the time, while the Canadian stroke returns halfway back under water, remaining in the water seventy-five per cent of the time. The J stroke brings the canoe back into line by the vertical position of the paddle blade in the water and a prying outward at right angles to the forward motion of the canoe. In the Canadian stroke, however, the paddle is parallel to the bottom of the canoe, and the down angling of the leading edge of the blade, with the water spilling over it, gives the purchase on the water, bringing the canoe into line by a prying up of the blade of the paddle. The Canadian stroke is more efficient because you lift the blade only fifty per cent of the return, creating no impediment to the forward motion of the canoe. The Canadian stroke is not only an excellent cruising stroke for all paddling, but it is a great racing stroke because of its forward-motion efficiency. It is the safer stroke, especially when paddling single from the center of the canoe.

One other forward stroke should be mentioned here and that is the Indian or hunting stroke. Here the principle of the Canadian stroke is used, only the paddle is completely returned under water. It is never taken from the water. This stroke is never used except in stalking game, in hunting or in photography, where the dripping of water would warn of your approach. It is a completely silent stroke. In the case of stalking, both bow and stern paddles are returned under water. It was well known to the Indians and our pioneer forefathers, where the slightest sound might have meant an arrow or musket ball in the back or a tomahawk sticking just above the ear.

To develop your cruising stroke, practice going a long way in a straight line. It is good to line up with some object in the distance and paddle a straight course. Remain on your knees. Keep your back and lower arm straight. Don't sway sideways, but rotate your body to get power, keeping your back vertical. Regulate your paddling to about thirty beats a minute. Keep your backward pull parallel to the center line of the canoe and don't scrape your paddle along the gunnel. Don't change sides. Use the weight of your shoulder and body for your forward drive—not your forearm. Use just enough steering in the stern to keep in line, and, above all, develop teamwork. Avoid horseplay in the canoe, and give care to landing and taking off. Once these things are accomplished, the turning or draw strokes are simple and easy, as are the jam or stopping strokes.

### Draw or Turning Strokes

The draw or turning strokes are quite simple and can be learned quickly. By draw strokes we mean side-pressing of the paddle either in toward the canoe, or pushing outward in order to change the canoe's direction by shoving or pulling it off a straight course. After the simple draws are learned, sculling will be taught. Sculling is a modified draw, where the tip of the paddle blade is rocked back and forth in the water in a semicircle with the pressure either in or out, drawing the canoe over toward the paddle by inward pressure, or pushing the canoe away from the paddle by outward pressure. The sweep stroke, used for long turns, is also a draw stroke. Each will be described. Sometimes the terms "out" and "in," in describing draw strokes, are confusing, so instead of using "out-draw" we will use the term "push-over" and for "in-draw" we will use the term "pull-over." Also, remember that the body stays in balance when it is vertical and low in the canoe, and that the reaching or pushing out is done mostly with the arms and some shoulder weight.

### Types of Draw Strokes

1. "Pull-over" or "in-draw"
2. "Push-over" or "out-draw"
3. Sculling in and out
4. Sweep strokes
5. Double hook for single paddling

Note: The cross-bow paddler and the bow rudder will be classified as jam strokes, but they are borderline strokes and there is some argument as to which group they belong in. To avoid confusion, we admit that they are a little of both, but they are more advanced strokes requiring considerable skill. Consequently, the author takes the privilege of putting them in a less frequently used group of strokes, allowing the beginner to use the simpler primary strokes for his first paddling practice.

PULL-OVER OR IN-DRAW    Draw strokes should first be practiced under the eye of an instructor, and the initial trys should be made by the beginner when the canoe is standing still, so their execution can be better understood. The pull-over or in-draw is made by turning the blade parallel to the center line of the canoe. The canoe will move toward the paddle by reaching the paddle out with the arms, keeping the body straight, then pulling in vertically to the canoe. This is used by both bow and stern paddlers. The combinations of strokes for turning will be outlined later in this chapter. One thing to remember on the "pull-over," especially when underway, is to pull the paddle vertically out of the water before the side of the canoe is reached. Otherwise you will find the canoe moving sideways toward the paddle and riding over it. Sometimes, with enough forward speed or current, this action will upset you or pull you out of the canoe. Old-timers call this "ketchen a crab." In moving forward the draws can be modified to any angle from parallel to the forward course of the canoe, to right angles. The greater the angle, the greater the change in direction or turn.

THE PUSH-OVER OR THE OUT-DRAW    The "push-over" or "out-draw" is executed in the exact reverse of the "pull-over" or "in-draw." The paddle is placed to the side of the canoe, parallel to the center, and is pushed outward, making the canoe move away from the paddle. When underway, either bow or stern can again use any angle from forward up to right angles according to the amount of turn required. When the canoe is standing still, it can be moved sideways by the bow using a push-over and the stern using a pull-over simultaneously. The canoe can be moved at right angles in the opposite direction by the bow using a pull-over and the stern using a push-over.

SCULLING    Sculling is important, especially in rapids or white water, as it is vital in split-second changes of direction. Therefore, the paddle is kept in the water. In-sculling is done by rocking the blade with the flat side toward the edge of the canoe and pressing toward the canoe. Out-sculling is done by pressing away from the canoe. Again, keep the blade away from the edge of the canoe and keep your body erect, using your arms for power, and as much weight from the shoulders as is possible without leaning out.

THE SWEEP STROKE   The sweep stroke is a type of draw for longer turns. The paddle blade is thrust forward by sliding the shaft through the lower hand until it is about a third of the way up. The paddle is then swung outward in a wide semicircle in the stern and a quarter circle in the bow. It is one of the easiest strokes to learn and the wider the reach the greater the turn. Due to the wider angle and reach, usually only about half of the blade is in the water. It is a pretty stroke and looks well in canoeing exhibitions. It is used constantly in paddling.

DOUBLE J STROKE   This is a stroke used only in single paddling, that is, where one person is handling the canoe. He is in the center, resting against the center thwart, down on his knees. The near edge of the paddle is twisted forward parallel to the center line of the canoe. An in-draw or pull-over is accomplished by reaching outward and forward, then pulling in a semicircle toward the canoe. The paddle, as it circles inward, is twisted at right angles to the center line of the canoe and the forward stroke is made and finished up by a hook or J on the end. This makes the canoe turn to the paddling side or execute an inward turn. The opposite turn of the canoe by a single man paddling on the same side is accomplished by a wide sweep. In fact, the double hook or J stroke is the opposite of the sweep stroke and results in a turn inward instead of outward from the side on which one is paddling.

## Jam Strokes and Stopping Strokes

Jam or stopping strokes act as brakes in canoeing. I have seen two big men come straight into the dock at full speed, suddenly thumb-locking their paddles to the gunnels with blades vertical and at right angles to the center line. This procedure causes the canoe to come to a sudden stop in less than its length. It takes close teamwork, good balance, a strong arm above and a strong thumb lock at the gunnel. The thumb lock is accomplished by holding the shaft of the paddle with the fingers, while hooking the thumb over the gunnel and holding fast. This should be practiced in open water until perfect before you try docking.

### Keel Lock

When entering or leaving a canoe you can steady it by a keel lock. The paddle is held tightly to the side of the canoe, vertical, with the blade parallel to the center line of the canoe. The shaft of the paddle should be thumb-locked to the gunnel. This adds a temporary keel to the canoe, and inward or outward pushes of the handle or grip will compensate for balance as does the umbrella of a tightwire walker. When the canoe is moving, the keel lock can be used occasionally like the centerboard in a sailboat in wind. If you are using a small sail on your canoe as is often done when the wind is favorable, and you want a rest from paddling a heavy load, the keel lock makes a fine substitute for a centerboard to prevent sideslipping in the wind.

### Stern Tiller or Rudder Lock

The above keel maneuver can be moved back to the stern of the canoe. The paddle locked in the crook of your arm becomes a tiller. By pulling the grip out or in, the canoe can be steered. This stroke can be used in sailing and will act both as a keel and a rudder, or it can be used in wide, deep, fast water where there is no danger of rocks and you want to loaf awhile, yet steer and keep control of the canoe. Be sure you're in safe water, though. In big rapids in the north, we went forty-eight miles in one morning using the rudder most of the way. It was always great fun.

### Bow Rudder

This is an advanced stroke for bow paddlers. It takes skill and certainly is not for beginners. It is especially effective in going upstream, but if not well executed it can turn over a canoe in the twinkling of an eye. To execute this stroke the bow paddler slides his lower hand up the shaft of the paddle, reaching with the blade vertical to the water, and places the tip of the blade several inches forward of the bow of the canoe with the blade flat against the bow. Then the paddler leans forward slightly, the grip hand is shoved across to the opposite shoulder and the blade is lowered into the water at an angle. The forward motion of the canoe immediately grabs hold of the tip of the blade and there is an immediate and often a violent change of direction opposite the paddling side of the bowman. This stroke also slows the forward motion of the canoe, acting like the flaps on an airplane. I once saw a man use this stroke while an outboard motor was driving along at a good clip, and it threw him completely out of the canoe. The results were certainly violent and startling.

### Cross-Bow Rudder

This is a much safer stroke than the bow rudder and can accomplish the same thing. The paddle is swung forward across the bow to the opposite side. The same hand position is retained. The paddle is thrust out at an angle from the bow of the canoe, the blade dipped in and pulled forward by the lower arm to the bow of the canoe. This stroke is used in emergencies, such as in rapids, and is a very valuable and effective turning-and-stopping stroke combination.

### Flamming

This stroke is mentioned more for information than use. It is used occasionally by highly skilled canoemen, in the Far North, in big white water that piles high. Without flamming, the canoe would be filled with foamy feather water. At the crucial moment, the bowman reaches forward with his paddle and vigorously sweeps it back and forth like a broom, directly in front of the bow, knocking a hole in the white water through which the canoe shoots. This takes skill, balance and great muscular power. Flamming is little known in our quieter waters.

### Single Paddling

A canoe is usually paddled by two paddlers, one in the bow and one in the stern. However, occasionally you go out alone. If the canoe is empty, kneel at the middle thwart, down on your knees, resting against the thwart. If you have duffel, balance up the weight by putting the load in the stern, and paddle facing it, resting against the forward thwart or bow seat. Keep the canoe on an even keel fore and aft, otherwise it will wind-vane and be very difficult to paddle. If the load is heavy enough to hold the canoe down, you can paddle from the stern seat or thwart. If there is head wind and your canoe is empty, sit forward of the center to keep the bow of the canoe down and the higher stern weather-vanes holding into the wind.

As to strokes, use the same ones the sternman uses in doubles. Use the J or hook or Canadian stroke for cruising in a straight line or the sweep or draw for turning. The only strictly single stroke is the double-hook or J stroke for sharp inside turns. Jam strokes and keel locks can be used as well as the cross-bow or rudder. Sculling is very effective in singles, especially in fast water. Single paddling is a little more strenuous, but it is great fun. Everyone should become proficient in single paddling, which teaches a lot about canoe-handling problems. If there is a mistake there is no argument as to whose fault it is.

### Reverse Paddling both Double and Single

Little need be said about reverse paddling as it is only occasionally that one has to back the canoe. If you use the same strokes in reverse, a little practice will teach you to back up. The distance is usually a few canoe lengths at the most, and there is only one important factor in reverse paddling; that is back sculling, which in big rapids is done by the sternman just enough to give way for steering. This will be explained in detail in river canoeing.

Remember that anyone can learn to paddle a canoe. Study the illustrations carefully. At the close of this chapter you will find a chart of stroke combinations for maneuvering a canoe, which will help a bow and stern team to practice strokes. A little study, a little practice and a little patience will turn you into a good canoeman. Good paddling!

*chapter 5*

# Lake or Sea Canoeing

After the fundamentals of canoe handling and paddling are mastered, it is usual to make a few short trips. Many go on to longer trips. Consequently, they soon find that there are three distinct and separate phases or areas of canoe travel, each with separate problems and different experiences. These are:

    1. Lake or open-water canoeing
    2. Down-river canoeing
    3. Up-river canoeing

Although the fundamentals of paddling, maneuvering and balance are the same, each area of experience requires special techniques and knowledge to meet its separate problem. Therefore, each phase is important, and will be treated in a separate chapter.

Lake canoeing involves knowledge of weather, simple navigation, wind, waves, fog, currents, finding of the passage and many other problems.

First of all, any wise guide or woodsman will tell you that only the foolhardy and the tenderfoot take unnecessary risks.

43

# CANOEING

There are enough inescapable risks in the everyday life of travel by canoe, especially in wild country, without deliberately going out unprepared on a large body of water. Without careful, calculated plans you may be inviting disaster.

Many times I have seen guides climb to a high rocky point and study a wide crossing of water for hours before starting for the other side. They note every feature on the sky line of the far shore, every current streak, every cloud in the sky, and the direction and variability of the wind. They watch the flight of the water birds, the action of the loons on the water, the tautness that has not left the tent rope even though the sun has been up at least an hour. They feel in the grass to see how fast the dew dries, watch for weather signs in the actions of the red squirrels and chipmunks. They even study the anthills to see if the ants are spreading out or concentrating on covering up their doorways with leaves.

An experienced woodsman, before crossing or venturing out on a large body of water, will notice all of the above things and more. Take, for instance, campfire smoke. If it rises lazily and goes straight up in the early morning, there will be no wind for at least three hours. If it wavers, spirals or breaks as it goes up, there is turbulence in the air preceding strong winds. If the smoke goes up a short piece and fans out over the water in a blanket, it means a falling barometer or rain. If it drops down on the surface it means possible fog and the necessity of blind navigation.

One studies the clouds for weather signs. High-flying cirrus clouds, often called "mackerel scales" or "mares' tails" by the sailors, denote rising winds, and the way they point usually indicates the direction from which the wind will blow. Large cumulus clouds warn of local squalls, which are dangerous on a large body of water. Keep a weather eye open when the cumulus or wool-packs are flying. Stratus clouds often mean rain or, if broken, rain and wind.

And so it goes, as weather lore becomes part of the wisdom necessary to living in a small boat on the open water. It is a fascinating study, increasing your respect for nature, giving you a humble feeling but building understanding of the Almighty and His manifold ways through nature. If you don't believe this, just get into a frail canoe alone in a big storm several miles from shore with darkness coming on. It takes the last bit of conceit out of you, leaving nothing but your skill and raw courage. Even though you are scared, a few prayers really help. I know—I've been there.

This little prelude is designed to give you the background of some of the problems of lake or large-water canoeing. They all simmer down to common sense, weather, wind, waves, and navigation. The techniques of heading into waves or going with the waves are similar, yet different in many respects. Going cross wind is a combination of both as you must tack back and forth when the waves get high.

## BREAKING THE WIND

Make use of all of the islands, headlands, and other obstructions to the wind, as it is wisdom to save your energy. Life is more enjoyable when you don't wear yourself out. If there are several canoes, keep them together and keep near land at all times unless a wide crossing is necessary. Then, be sure of your weather and be prepared for emergencies. Plot a calculated course in advance of a wide crossing. Tie in and cover your duffel with canvas and fasten your map and compass in front of you. Above all, keep your party of canoes in line or abreast in quiet water and set the pace according to the speed of the slowest canoe. Allow no straggling; keep together. Talk over and agree on line position and create a plan for any possible emergencies. The guide is usually the lead canoe, and the next in authority brings up the rear, allowing no one to drop behind. Most accidents occur because of stragglers, as they usually are the least skilled and exhibit the least team-work.

With the foregoing as a background, let us spend a typical day on the big water together. Usually there is no wind until the sun has been up for two or three hours. If it is blowing briskly early in the morning, you had better stay in camp and do some fishing off shore in the lee of the wind, or repair equipment or just loaf. One time I was wind-bound for three and one half days on a small island. Two years later two prospectors took out thirty-five thousands dollars in gold from beneath our campfire site, but that is another story.

First, study the weather and your map. Then, plot your course for the day. All of your party should be in on this for their own satisfaction and morale. All canvas should be dry before packing if possible. Once packed up, with duffel tied in and covered with canvas, the camp site should be thoroughly cleaned. The fire should be completely out. Instructions for the day are in order when the canoes are all ready. Course, position in line and a word about the possibilities of weather are outlined. The canoes shove off, the guide leading.

There is a tendency in the morning, especially for the less experienced, to try to paddle fast. The wise guide will set a steady pace of about thirty beats per minute and rest five minutes out of every half hour, stopping for a somewhat longer period about the middle of the morning to stretch and fish. In Canada, a bucket of tea is usually made. At least an hour at noon should be taken for lunch with another break in the middle of the afternoon for tea. Rub olive oil on the hands at each stop to prevent blisters until the hands toughen up and become like fine, oil-tanned leather.

At the beginning of a trip, go easy on the paddling until you get into shape. Plan your itinerary so that the easiest part is at the beginning, allowing those who are new to learn to handle and paddle a canoe. Start your trip in the lakes and end up through the rivers if possible, as the latter are usually more difficult.

### Paddling into Waves and Headwinds

Probably the major problems of canoe travel on lakes, especially big lakes, are weather, wind and waves. First of all, as has been advised, use every possible island, point and headland as a

windbreak. Plot your course so that you can move up in the lee of a windbreak, thereby saving time and energy. This should be done even if it increases paddling distance.

When a group of canoes are moving upwind, and the waves begin to roll up, the lead canoe should be followed tandem style by the others, who thus take advantage of the breaking of the waves by the lead canoe. In case of a crossing several miles wide, canoes can take turns leading, and breaking the wind and waves for the rest of the line.

Do not drive into waves at right angles, but quarter a little. The wind actually helps you to go forward. This is the same principle as beating up close to the wind in a fore- and aft-rigged sailing boat.

As waves get larger, there must be careful timing between the bow and stern paddler. As the wave reaches the bow, the stern paddler scoops down hard in the water with a heavy forward stroke that has a tendency to lift up the end of the canoe and steady it on the impact of the wave. Skillfully done, this helps to prevent shipping water. The bowman holds his paddle until the crucial moment. He then makes a quick stroke, just after the wave strikes the bow, to keep control and prevent heeling or weather-vaning. This is very important, for when the canoe is on the exact crest of a wave it is often hard for both paddlers to reach the water, and a gust of wind can flip the canoe around, rolling it over in the twinkling of an eye. Keep your paddle in the water as much as possible, especially when riding the crest of a wave. Unfortunately, when making a crossing in wind and wave there is no opportunity to rest; consequently, a slow steady pace is best. Stick to it until you are across. Stopping for five minutes is not only dangerous, but can often cost you an hour's hard work. The best advice is: don't get out in big water when the waves are too high.

In tidal lakes, rivers, basins and bays you also have the tide to contend with. If the tide comes in against the wind, you will find yourself in dangerous choppy seas. If it is with the wind, you had better head for the nearest land and wait until conditions are favorable.

## Paddling with the Wind and Waves

If the waves are small and the wind light, it is a pleasure to have a tail wind. We would often put up a half pup tent or cut a balsam fir and use it for a sail. By sitting in the bottom of the canoe and steering one can often ride for miles. We covered seventy-two miles in one day that way on a long narrow lake in the Far North. It is great fun, but keep your weight low and be ready for instant release of your sail in case of a sudden squall.

When the waves get to be over a foot high, showing a tendency to break, and the sea under you begins to heave up, it becomes an entirely different matter. Again the problem of vaning at the top of the wave is a danger, even more than going into the wind, due to your increased speed. The prolonged forward rush of the top of the wave will have a tendency to turn you because, at crest, the speed of the water at the back end of the canoe is faster, and the bow is nosing into the backslip or undertow in slower water. Keep paddling, keep forward speed, and watch the dangerous tendency to heel. If the water gets too rough, head for the nearest land and stay there until it is safe. Make certain that the canoes stay several lengths apart. A big wave can pick up a canoe and throw it on top of the one ahead caught by the undertow. Keep at least three canoe lengths away or paddle abreast.

## Riding out a Storm

A canoe can withstand an amazing amount of rough weather, but don't get caught if you can possibly prevent it, because riding out a storm is not child's play. Stay off the water if there is danger of a big storm. However, if you do get caught, try to keep cool even though you are scared stiff. Remain low and keep your paddle going as long as possible. Reach land if you can. If you can't, ride out the storm. Don't fight it, go with it. You may end up fifty miles away, but no storm blows forever. Try to keep your bearings, and calculate your possible drift speed and its direction.

The chapter on canoe safety will tell you what to do if a canoe is swamped or upset.

If a canoe should upset when you are alone on a calm lake, roll it upright, ride down on the stern and kick hard until the forward motion of the canoe causes the bottom to plane upward and spills out a few inches of the water. Then go alongside, and bail, using your hands or hat or boot until you can get aboard and finish the job. If there are other canoes use the canoe rescue. (*See chapter on canoe safety.*)

If you are alone and the canoe swamps, as in a storm, you may stay aboard or go over the side, but *stay with the canoe*. It will float and save your life.

## Lake Navigation

A full explanation of lake navigation can be found in the book, *Canoe Camping*, by the author, published by A. S. Barnes and Company. Have the best maps available, especially on big lakes full of islands. I know of one lake that has islands with lakes on them, which in turn have islands that also have lakes. It can become quite complicated. Besides maps, have a good compass and give an eye to your directions at all times. Lay out a course and then keep to it. Watch an object in the distance, and keep the bow of the canoe in line with it.

Calculate your speed, compensating for head or tail winds or

currents. Every so often look back to your starting point, and then ahead to see if you are in line with your goal. This is known as hindsighting and is used by all navigators, sailors and woodsmen.

Lake canoeing is great fun and moreover, it combines a knowledge of paddling, navigation, and weather lore with common sense. Take it steady, rest regularly and learn to relax. Sing a song, and have a good time. Canoeing is not only a practical and efficient means of travel, but it can offer carefree hours full of compensation. It increases understanding of the elements of nature in God's great out of doors.

*chapter 6*

# Down-River Canoeing

Down-river canoeing is canoeing at its best. The current is with you; each bend is a new adventure. You will derive varied and exciting experiences from this type of canoeing.

You will have most of the problems of lake canoeing plus a greater need for paddling skill. You will use guiding strokes more, as most rivers swing back and forth and so require turning, twisting, quick change of direction and a fine understanding of navigation. In addition to the above there are the problems of fast and slow currents. It will be safer on the river than on the lake in wind and bad weather. On the other hand, you will study the currents, learn about bars and undercut banks, how to avoid obstructions and other things not found in lake canoeing. A careful study of your course through the swift waters and rapids will be part of your training. You must learn how to pick the channel, and the safe way between rocks through fast water or rapids. In shallower fast water you may have to resort to snubbing with a pole (putting on the brakes) or in the worst places to letting down with a rope. If the rapids are big or if there is a waterfall you will find it necessary to portage or carry your canoe and gear around. If there

51

is any question about rapids, never take a risk, especially in wild country.

You will find that besides knowledge of the river, the major factor in river canoeing is teamwork between the bow and stern paddlers and their knowledge of the paddling strokes such as the hook, Canadian, sweep, draw, bow rudder, and cross-bow rudder, sculling and jam strokes. All will be used, and both bow- and sternman will, after practice, almost automatically throw the correct strokes without a word, the only signal being the movement of the bowman as interpreted by the sternman. It is marvelous to see two veteran woodsmen negotiate difficult water. They will paddle for hours through treacherous fast water and rips without a word passing between them. They ride a canoe as we ride a bicycle or drive a car through heavy traffic. It becomes almost automatic, yet they learn the art of relaxing between efforts that require strength and skill. You, too, can become skilled and efficient, but take plenty of time and practice to learn. Never run risks and always look ahead, picking out the course and laying a plan of action for likely problems. Be on the alert for emergencies, especially in fast water, and practice teamwork with your paddling partner. Now let us consider the various types of rivers, from slow streams to fast waters, and the problems and techniques involved.

*Slow Current*

When the river is slow, swinging lazily in wide, meandering curves, it is usually found to be silty or sandy. On the inside of the curve there is usually a shelving sand or silt bar that drops gently away. The rivermen call this the "barside," while the outside of the curve, where the current is stronger, is the undercut bank or the deep side and is known to rivermen as the "bankside." In traveling downstream one will find that the faster current is usually near the bankside while the water across the point or bar is usually sluggish. The twisting and turning of the river calls for constant turning and guiding of the canoe, using sweeps, draws and occasionally a bow rudder or cross-bow rudder on the tighter bends. Downstream paddling affords excellent paddling practice.

A study of the banks of a stream often gives a clue to the contour of the bottom. If the bank is steep, the stream is usually deep.

A flat slope to the bank usually means a shelving bar reaching out into the stream. You will soon learn that the high banks are first on one side and then on the other, following the current which swings back and forth. The same holds true for the shelving bars or points. You will find them first on one side and then on the other.

It is best to stay about two thirds of the width of the stream away from the points and about one third from the undercut banks. Logs and obstructions are usually encountered near the undercut banks, while the sand or silt bars and slower waters delay forward speed and increase the chances of running aground.

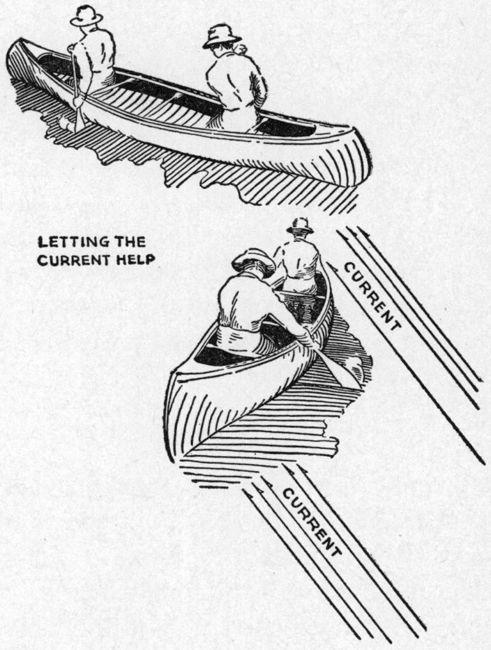


At this point the old and well-known trick of increasing your speed and saving physical effort by quartering into the current should be mentioned. As you pass a point, the canoe should be pulled into such position that the current quarters on the stern. This is the same principle as sailing up close before the wind in a fore- and aft-rigged sailboat, except that the impulse on your canoe is the push of the current quartering on your stern. It actually pushes your canoe forward at a surprising speed with little paddling effort. As soon as you approach the next undercut bank, pull the stern of your canoe back over and catch it on the other quarter. Tack back and forth across the current, keeping to the channel. Avoid getting too close to the undercut bank or the shelving points. Stay in the current, and by tacking, you will make a great many miles in one day with a minimum of effort.

*Stream Navigation*

At this point we shall digress for a bit to bring up the problem of navigation, which involves remaining aware at all times of your position on the map. First of all, on a river it is important

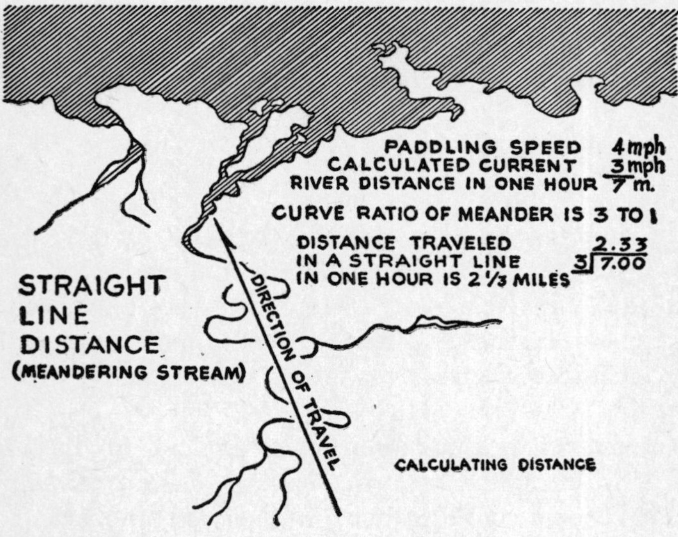


to know your forward speed plus the speed of the current. As rivers meander or swing back and forth, sometimes for miles across a big valley, it is also essential to calculate your straight-line distance. Usually the beginner will be amazed at the long distances traveled on a meandering stream to accomplish only a few straight-line miles on the map. A guide or canoe leader should always give his party instruction on some of the problems of river navigation and let them study the calculated progress. He should teach them to watch the sun, the direction of the shadows, the drift of the clouds or such landmarks as a big hill or mountain ahead. It is necessary to understand that the usual ratio of meandering stream distance to forward straight-line distance is usually about three miles of stream to one mile straight line. A thirty-beat-per-minute stroke will take you about four miles in one hour. Keep track of the time it takes for a chip or stick to float one hundred feet in the fastest current and multiply by 52.8 to get the amount of time it takes the current to float the chip one mile. Let us say that the current is estimated at three miles per hour, you are paddling four miles per hour, and the ratio is three to one of the meandering stream. The straight-line distance on your map is calculated as follows:

> Paddling speed      4 miles per hour
> Current speed      3 miles per hour
> Total river distance      7 miles
> 7 miles river distance: 3 (ratio of meander-
>              ing stream)
> equals 2.33 miles covered in a straight line
>              on the map.

It is very important to know this as most maps do not mark the meandering of a stream, and the uninformed often become greatly confused, discouraged or lost. Navigation is not only necessary, but it is fun and it should be taught to everyone in your party. It is good education and gives everyone an understanding of what is going on.

Don't depend on winds for a clue to direction on meandering streams! It is all right to use sun, shadows, cloud drift and your compass in keeping your direction, but the wind often swings with the valleys and rivers. This can especially be noted from the air when you fly over a meandering slow stream in an airplane.

## Finding the Channel in Very Slow or Flooded Streams

Often in big sluggish streams or on those that are flooded by a dam, it is difficult to follow the channel. There are several ways of finding the direction of the current and the channel. In flood season, watch for driftwood piles that point the direction of the flow of water. The tiny pin minnows head upstream and usually stay to the channel. One of the best indicators of the direction of the current and channel is the tape grass which points down the current. If the flooded area is in a forest, watch for the open path through the drowned trees. Use your map and compass to get the general direction of the flow. Also watch out for obstructions and stubs because they are often hard to locate in sluggish water.

*Paddling in Faster Water*

An old friend of mine, Andy Anderson, observed, while holding his handle-bar moustache out of the tea he was drinking, that "the difference between slow and fast water is that you have less time to think." A sudden snow squall had driven us off the river and while we waited for it to pass, we were crouching in the shelter of the huge roots of an uprooted pine. We were trying to get out of the "bush" before the spirits of the north wind swept down to rule the realms of the great north forests with a hand of frosty steel. The river was fast water and we waited for the curtain of snow to sweep on, leaving its magic stippling over the jackpines, spruce and balsam fir as it marched away toward the purple mountains in the distance. Andy was right: thinking processes must speed up with the water.

If you have been traveling in a wide, sweeping sandy river, one of the surest signs of coming swift water is the appearance of rocks along the sides and an occasional riffle. The hills or mountains usually come in closer and the river begins to straighten out so that you can see reaches of it, sometimes for a quarter of a mile or more. The gradient, or the increased slope of the stream, causes the water to flow faster. Usually it is more shallow, and rocks and logs become an increased problem as the speed of the current increases.

A word should be said here about recognition of underwater obstructions. Most underwater obstructions leave a telltale mark on the surface of the stream. You should study the water for at least one hundred yards in advance and pick a path through obstructions, keeping to the safe waters. Even in fast water the river has a tendency to swing from one side to another. Consequently, you should follow the channel of the deepest flow of the water. An obstruction underwater splits the current, forming a "V" pointing upstream. Avoid it! A swirl in the center of the "V" tells how deep the obstruction is under the water. Rounded boulders cause the stream to heave upward. Sharp stones split the current and

give a boiling look to the rapids. Underwater ledges often cause the current to turn sharply right or left. These can be especially dangerous. Take it easy and slow down in the worst spots. Pick your course between the "V's," keeping to the deeper water.

The bowman must be especially vigilant because he must dictate the course if there is an obstruction of any kind immediately in front of the canoe. However, the sternman is in charge and picks the course at least one hundred yards in advance. Use a regular cruising stroke, keep enough headway for steering and, of course, use the draws and sculling for change of course or direction.

When it comes to short rapids, chutes and other swift waters, one canoe "shoots through" before the next enters. On short rapids this prevents "piling up" in case of an accident in the canoe ahead. Once I saw three canoes pile up in one short rapids, and loss in cameras alone amounted to over one thousand dollars.

If there is any doubt about a rapids, portage around it. The old-timers always do. That's why they have lived to be old-timers.

The guide, on approaching a rapids where the water above is fairly quiet, usually has the bowman keel his paddle to steady the canoe. Then he carefully stands up, keeping toes in and center for balance, and studies the rapids ahead, analyzing obstructions, the lay of the current and the channel. He instructs the rest of the canoes and leads off, with each canoe waiting for the one ahead to complete the run of the rapids before starting through.

When approaching the top of a rapids, do not paddle in at

full speed. Veteran woodsmen approach slowly and take good aim. Study and plot your course, talk detail with your bowman, and get just enough headway to keep steerage.

In the more difficult rapids, the bowman throws his steering strokes while the sternman often back sculls or "fishtails." Expert canoemen, such as the French and the Indians, actually go down the rapids slower than the speed of the water. With powerful back sculling or fishtailing they are able to steer by sculling the canoe backward up the current. This takes a lot of experience and strong shoulders and arms. It is a beautiful sight to see veteran woodsmen negotiating a big rapids. They will drop down at a surprising speed, and seem to poise when complicated and difficult obstructions appear. They hover like hawks, move over into position by back sculling and then shoot down again. This is canoeing at its best. However, if you are a beginner, carry around the more difficult water and use your draw, sweep and cruising strokes through small swifts or rapids. Again, *if there is the least doubt, carry around*. If there is the least danger, one man should stand by the edge with a coil of rope ready for rescue. This precaution may save not only your buddies, but also precious grub and equipment.

### Snubbing

Often a stream will slope down like a tin roof for miles and will be too dangerous to paddle down, yet will offer no opportunity for carrying. I know one such stretch sixty-five miles in length. Usually a stream is shallower in these stretches and is best negotiated by snubbing. When such water is reached, stop and cut a good three-hand pole about ten feet long. Spruce is best, but birch will do, although it is heavier. Smooth it so no stubs will tear your hands. There should be a pole for each canoe.

When a difficult area is approached, the bowman steadies the canoe as the sternman stands up and braces one leg against the thwart on the side of the bow paddler, with the other leg back in a good comfortable stance. He poles along until the swift water begins, while the bowman keeps up a regular stroke. When the swift water begins, the pole is gently thrust forward at a forty-five degree angle until a good purchase or grip is obtained on the bottom. Pressure is applied on the pole forward and downward, and the canoe begins to slow down as a car does when the brakes are

used. This is known as snubbing. Do not get your pole too near the side of the canoe or you might have difficulty and "ketch a crab." The canoe can be guided by reaching out with your arm and pressing down on the pole which, like the pull-over draw, pulls the canoe toward the pole. Or, if the pole is swung inward, the canoe will move away from the pole as in a push-over draw. It is not necessary to completely stop the canoe, although you can stop it dead still even in very fast water. The object of snubbing, however, is to slow the canoe in order to guide it through difficult water. Snubbing is usually done in the shallower waters. It is fascinating sport and takes real skill, but anyone can do it with practice. Start out in the easier stretches until you become accomplished enough to try the bigger ones.

Another way of slowing down in smaller, gravel-bottom swift water is "dragging." The pole is placed back at a forty-five degree angle, and held under the near arm while the other arm pushes upward. The pole drags on the bottom, acting as a brake. However, this is not to be used in the faster or more difficult stretches of water, for you do not have the control of the canoe that you have by snubbing.

*Tracking or Letting Down with a Rope*

When water gets too deep or dangerous for snubbing and there is no chance to portage, the only other alternative is to let down with a rope. Every canoe should carry not less than fifty feet of strong one-quarter or three-eighths manila rope. As a difficult stretch of water is approached, the canoes should be brought to the shore and all duffel tied down securely under a covering of canvas. Each canoe must be haltered by a good rope. One end of the rope is tied to the thwart just in front of the sternman, and the other end is tied to the front thwart or front seat. The bowman walks along the shore with the pole while the sternman handles the ropes. The canoe is shoved out into the stream by the pole until it is caught by the current. When the bow rope is pulled, the stern of the canoe angles outward, catching the current and moving toward the center of the stream. When you want to move the canoe toward shore, pull on the stern rope, the canoe angles on the other tack, and the current pushes it inshore. It is an interesting sight to see a canoe being guided down a stream, often twenty-five or thirty feet out from shore, guided around obstructions by remote control from the man on shore who is letting it down. A sure sign of a tenderfoot is a canoeman wading while letting a canoe down. It is so much easier, safer and drier to let down by a rope.

*Portaging*

Portages in canoe country are usually marked. However, if you are going into wild country, be sure to have good maps and a guide who knows the territory. Many times portages start up in quiet water, so begin to look before you reach fast water. More often they are just at the top of the dangerous water, consequently, come in carefully, take care in landing and use caution in unloading. Canoes and gear should be carried up out of the water at once and prepared for transportation. Portaging will be taken up in detail later in chapter eight.

As a closing observation on down-river canoeing, it should be said that streams vary in size and gradient and each has its particular problems. This variation is what makes canoeing such an interesting sport. You do not have to go into the Far North to get excited about canoeing. Just try a trip down the upper Delaware river, the Beaverkill of New York, the New River of West Virginia, the Kentucky River, or the Niangua in the Ozarks. You can acquire some wonderful experience and store up many unforgettable memories.

## chapter 7

# Up-River Canoeing

Traveling upstream in a canoe is an entirely different problem from either downstream canoeing or canoeing on lakes or other large waters. When understood properly, the technique of going upstream is not difficult. Of course, in the canoe country of Canada one often has to go upstream for many miles, pushing heavy loads. When possible on the very long rapids, like the forty-mile rapids of the Mississangi, one would cut across the bush, carrying from lake to lake. This is not often possible, however, so let us compare up-river with down-river canoeing.

First of all, in down-river canoeing you have the current with you and the object is to slow down in the worst places and keep away from rocks, logs and other obstructions. In up-river canoeing you have the current against you. The problem, therefore, is not one of slowing down but of going up faster than the current. The rocks and obstructions are your friends. You pull up behind them for they break the current. In coming downstream you are going with the current and your paddle strokes do not get as great a purchase on the water because the water is moving with you. But in up-river canoeing your craft is alive and sensitive to any guiding stroke as the water is speeding by you. Instead of lying sluggish in the current, as is often the case in down-river canoeing, swift water is like a headstrong, half-wild horse that wants to spin about and plunge in the other direction. Canoeing upstream is a fascinating problem, challenging one's knowledge and skill. I suggest that you read the section on up-river canoeing in *Canoe Camping* by the author for a description of the great odds that can be overcome by a canoe even in the wildest kind of water.

## Up-River Canoeing on Wide, Quiet Rivers

In paddling up a wide, meandering or twisting stream the problem is somewhat the same as in down-river canoeing except that you come up behind the shelving points, thereby taking ad-

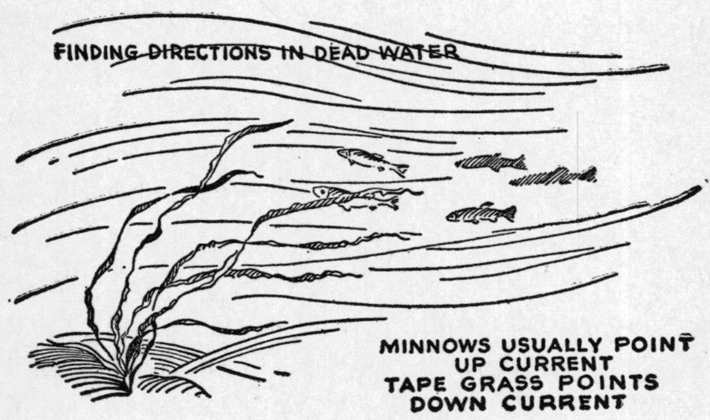


vantage of the slower water. Again you can use the current to help you upstream by tacking back and forth from one shelving point to another. The current, pushing at an angle at the side of a canoe, actually helps you to go upstream and saves fifty per cent of the energy required to hit the current head on (*see drawings*). You consequently move up faster, go farther, and are less tired at night. Try to conserve energy at all times, especially with a heavy load, as you will get enough exercise in eight hours of paddling.

The question of women paddling upstream should be answered at this point. Women often become more skillful in handling a canoe than men. A man has a tendency to fight the current, using "bull strength," while a woman will often study the easier ways of doing the job and develop skill in paddling and poling to offset her lack of physical strength. I have seen men exhausted by nighttime, while the women come through with enough energy left to help with the cooking and dishes. It gives us males a little pause for thought.

*Navigation Upstream*

In going upstream the problems of navigation are similar to those met going downstream, but the estimated speed of the current, allowing about a one-third reduction of the slower current behind the points and the back water, is subtracted from instead of added to the forward speed of the canoe. The meandering of an average stream is about three miles of stream to one mile straight line on the map. Your straight-line map distance would be calculated as follows:

| | |
|---|---|
| Speed of current of river | 3 miles per hour |
| One third saved by using back water | –1 mile per hour |
| Total current | 2 miles per hour |
| | |
| Paddling speed | 4 miles per hour |
| Less current speed | –2 miles per hour |
| River distance | 2 miles per hour |

Meandering ratio equals 1:3 or straight-line distance equals two miles river distance divided by three, equals two thirds of a mile straight line on the map in one hour.

One of the big problems for newcomers in canoeing, especially in wild country, is that they think they have gone much farther in a straight line than they actually have. After a portage, however, they always seem to prefer paddling even if it is upstream and slow work.

It is important to relax when paddling. Any prize fighter will tell you that fights are won by the ability to concentrate energy on a blow and then to relax immediately. The same principle is used in canoeing. Going upstream is like battling a head wind on the open water. You have to time your stroke as a prize fighter times his punch, then relax as you swing your paddle and pole. It is a must on any trip, even with professional bushmen, prospectors or Hudson's Bay brigades, to stop and rest at least ten minutes out of every hour and make tea in midmorning and midafter-

noon. But the greatest rest is that taken between strokes. Strong men, who are tycoons in business, learn more about relaxing by paddling upstream in the canoe country than all their expensive doctors can teach them. I have many friends who say that the secrets of relaxation learned in a canoe were carried back to their desks, preventing high blood pressure and ulcers, adding joy to work and years to their lives. If you are on a pleasure trip in a canoe, take time to relax, stop at the good fishing spots, have fun and avoid taking people with you who have to run on a schedule. Nature knows no schedule except sunrise, sunset and change of seasons. Enjoy yourself, and when you have to paddle upstream be philosophical; plug along and enjoy it. It's a little slower, but it can be an interesting game and a challenge to skill. You'll get there eventually.

## Poling

As a stream gets swifter and straightens out so you can no longer take advantage of the quiet water behind the shelving points—especially if the stream shallows so that the paddle strikes bottom—then is the time to use a pole. Land and cut two poles of good strong light wood such as spruce. Trim them carefully, remove all stubs and smooth them down with your knife. At first, on streams that are not too swift, the bowman continues to paddle while the sternman uses the pole. The bow paddle should be used on the same side as the pole, because it is easier for the bow to use a pull-over draw than a push-over draw, and the added force of the pole gives better control if the "bow" paddles on the same side as the sternman poles.

The poler in the stern stands carefully with his leg opposite the poling side braced forward comfortably against the thwart. The knees should be slightly bent and the foot toe in to give an easy balance. The leg nearest the poling is back center and toe in. When he has a good comfortable stance, he grasps his pole and tests his balance like a tightwire walker.

Poling is: (1) the stance with the sharpened pole ready, (2) the cast or the reach forward with the pole at a forty-five degree angle, (3) the catch or purchase on the bottom of the stream as the canoe moves forward (4) the drive which shoots the canoe forward.

The pole is ten feet long and the hand uses three grips as the pole drives the canoe forward. This is why the ten-foot pole is called the three-hand pole. (It is interesting to note that the French song "Alouette" is a poling, not a paddling song, as is popularly believed. The four-beat cadence represents the four movements of poling the stance and three hands on the drive.)

I drove a canoe in Kentucky up over a dam with a twenty-degree pitch, using a pole, and won several bets. The people thought it was impossible, although their fellow Kentuckians in Eastern Kentucky two hundred miles away pole "Joe Boats" up rapids every day and think nothing of it.

Guiding the canoe with a pole is quite simple. First of all, keep the pole six inches to a foot out from the gunnel. To make the canoe move in the direction opposite the poling side the pole is swung in at an angle toward the side of the canoe as the drive forward is made. The stern will move away from the pole, and the bow will move in the opposite direction, making the turn toward the poling side. To move the canoe toward the pole reach out until the pole angles outward away from the canoe. Then, when the drive is made, the canoe will move toward the pole. This maneuver turns the bow of the canoe away from the poling side and is used for both bow and stern poling.

In moving upstream with a pole astern and paddle in the bow, use every obstruction that splits the current and come up in the center of the V behind them. You will find a considerable backwash behind the larger obstructions. I have watched an experienced canoeman, who desired a little breather or rest, push his canoe up behind a big boulder, splitting the current, then calmly put pole and paddle aboard while the eddy or backwater holds the canoe up behind the rock in the midst of a roaring rapids. Then he takes out his pipe and has a smoke while the rapids growl and roar around him.

We often do this while fishing, especially for trout which lazy around the swirls behind boulders watching for food to float by. It is great and exciting sport, especially when your speckled trout get up to around three or four pounds. The action of the trout plus the action of the roaring water means fishing at its best.

### Two-Man Poling

As the stream gets swifter it will require that both bow- and sternman pole. Again, pole on the same side, taking a good comfortable stance and using very close teamwork. The bow poler holds the canoe with his pole in the bottom. Then, as the sternman begins his drive, the bowman follows, timing his drive just a little after the sternman. As the canoe shoots forward, the bowman's pole is ready to hold bottom as soon as the canoe loses its head speed, allowing the stern poler to get another purchase on the bottom for another drive upward. This holding by the bowman is necessary to keep the nose of the canoe into the current. Otherwise, it would turn in a flash. By drawing in or out with the pole the canoe can be turned right or left, shoved broadside right or

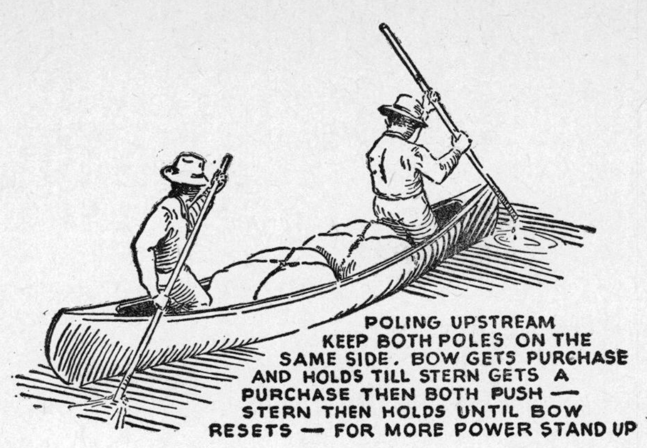



left, or spun around either way. Poling is great fun and it can be practiced in quieter waters before venturing into rapids. When proficient enough, you can pole up through very fast water, particularly if you come up behind rocks or other obstructions. If you are going to canoe extensively, especially carrying a load, a knowledge of poling is indispensable. It is your low gear for the steep grades.

## Tracking

When the stream is too deep to pole, or perhaps too swift, tracking upstream with a rope will be necessary. It will be the reverse of the process of tracking described in the chapter on down-river canoeing. A fifty-foot or more quarter-inch manila rope is attached to the forward thwart by the gunnel on the side on which you are going to pull. The other end is attached to the thwart just in front of the stern paddler. The rope on the same side looping ashore is operated by one paddler while the other walks ahead with the pole to fend off the canoe in the close and more difficult places. Pulling on either bow or stern will cause the quartering current to turn the canoe out or inshore.

In the worst places a second fifty-foot rope is sometimes attached to the ring on the front of a canoe. If you have a third party have him walk up ahead on the shore pulling on the single rope at the more critical places while the double-attached rope controls the steering. Occasionally in narrow fast waters I have seen ropes attached on each side and a man pulling from each shore. It is also a common practice in the big rivers of the Far

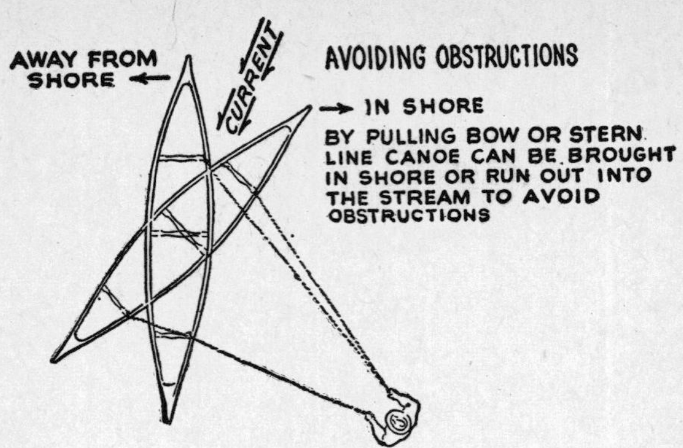


North for one man to stay aboard with a pole to push and guide the canoe while the other takes a single rope attached to the front thwart. Tracking is desirable for long reaches of fast water where it is difficult to portage. If the water is dangerous and the shore line is not conducive to walking, you had better pack up and portage around if you can.

Up-river canoeing is fun. It is a fascinating game of wits and skill. It can provide breath-taking moments and you will, in time, know both defeat and the sweet taste of victory over the river. The half-wild bushmen that I have traveled with over the years still leave an offering of tobacco to the Winabashoo, the mighty woods spirit, so he will help, or at least not hinder them, when they venture forth on the roaring, foaming breast of a mighty river with paddle, pole and rope. Try it! It's great sport. There is nothing like up-river canoeing.

## chapter 8

# Canoe Portaging and Gear

An old Swedish friend of mine once observed that canoeing is different from any other water travel because on almost any trip for part of the time you travel *under* your boat. What he meant was that occasionally you have to portage or carry it around some impassable part of a stream or from one body of water to another. These carries or portages vary from a few yards to a few miles. In the Far North, a day on a portage equals about ten miles. If a

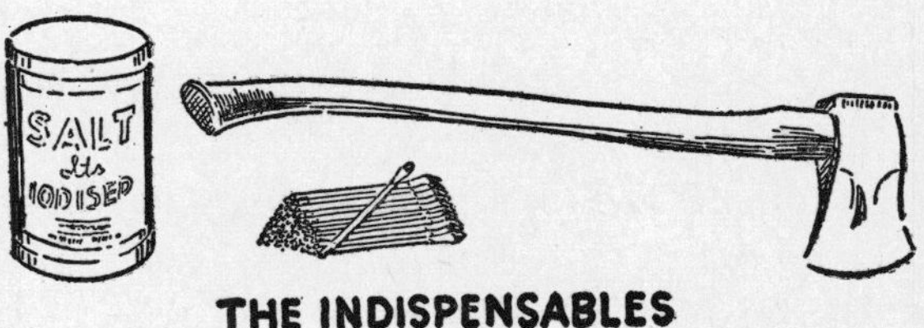


**THE INDISPENSABLES**

portage is marked "three days," it means thirty miles' carry and so on. However, these distances are not for tourists, who should avoid too tough a country. Such portages are found in remote and lonely country and are used only by Indians and a few white men who are native or professional. It takes a lot of experience and conditioning to walk ten miles under a canoe in one day, especially in fly or mosquito season. I know—I've done it. It is not recommended for pleasure.

The usual portage, however, will average from two hundred and fifty to one thousand yards. A portage sometimes is a mile or two long, seldom more. When planning a trip, try to avoid the rough, long portages. It often pays to go a little farther around to miss some tough portages. However, portages are often a necessary part of canoeing.

*Maps*

The first requisites for locating portages are good maps. Aerial maps are the best, but they are usually under government restriction and not often available. In the wilderness areas Forestry Service maps are the best, and in Canada good maps can be obtained by writing to the Provincial Departments of Lands and Forests. It is well to carry maps, as they make your trip far more interesting and educational, and also help in navigation. The conservation departments and forestry departments of each of the states of the United States have maps.

You will find in both Canada and the United States, where mining and stratigraphical geological maps are available, that mining cartographers are usually more accurate than most map makers in the mapping of the rivers, lakes and other bodies of water. Your outfitter usually has maps and can give you good information and advice. Also, your guide usually has maps of most routes—or can get them. Be careful of maps made by other than professional people; they may be out of scale and often are inaccurate and confusing.

When you are cruising in your canoe, fasten your map on

your duffel ahead of you so that you can constantly refer to it. Tie your compass to the gunnel with a strong piece of line. This line should be a few feet long, permitting the compass to be placed on the map and leveled up so the needle is free to point.

Constantly orient yourself, watch for landmarks, watch the

sun and shadow, the direction of the wind, the cloud drift, and use the age-old woodsman's trick of hindsighting or looking back occasionally. Hindsighting helps you to keep on course and makes landmarks familiar in case you have to backtrack. Constant vigilance, checking compass and map, watching for changes in course, and memorizing outstanding landmarks are all part of locating your route.

## Locating the Portage

In large lakes, use your maps and above-mentioned techniques in finding your way. Usually the best way to find the exit from a lake is to watch the sky line. There is usually a notch in the sky line if there are hills, or in the timber if the country is flat. Except in very remote country, portages are usually marked. In case there are no cut trails, land carefully, blaze your way and select the best route to the next lake or river before you cut your trail. Then clear out all the major obstructions and overhanging branches. Blaze your trail both ways so your party won't get lost. If you locate the portage trail and you are not sure that it is the right one, take an axe to clear obstructions and walk over it before you make the carry. This often saves you effort and error.

### Landing and Preparing to Portage

Once the portage is definitely located, land the canoes carefully, safely stow the duffel on shore, then carry the canoes up a few yards so the rest of your party can land. Stow duffel and gear

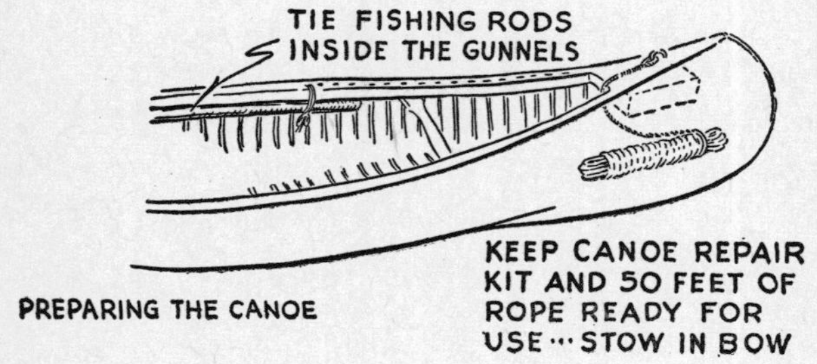


in one open place, as it is easy to lose things on the trail. Also remember that fifty per cent of canoe damage is done on the portage. Be sure that everything is secure and ready before you start across.

### Protection of Canoe and Gear on the Portage Trail

If on a long portage in wild country you cannot carry everything at once, it may be necessary to leave some of your equipment at either end of the portage for a considerable length of time. Cache it up in a tree or cut three poles to make a tripod from which to suspend your gear—especially food—by a rope so

it is out of reach of bears, porcupines, chipmunks, red squirrels and mice. Bears, especially, seem to hang around the ends of portage trails where people are likely to camp or cook. "Moqua" the bear, who is always an opportunist, may tear up your gear and get away with your food. If possible, leave someone to watch. Of course, in civilization, it is often to prevent fellow men from looting. In Michigan once, I came back just in time to see a motorist putting my equipment in the back of his car. I don't know whether he was dishonest or not. He claimed that he thought someone had lost it, and he was picking it up, hoping to find the owner.

## Preparation for Carrying Your Canoe

The canoe is usually carried by one man. For the longer carries the paddles should be tied into a "paddle yoke" (*see illustration*). As soon as the canoe is safely out of the water, the sternman gets ready to carry it while the bowman stows and prepares the duffel for transportation. The paddle blades are placed on the center thwart and tied about four inches apart in the middle of the center thwart. The ties can be left permanently in place and the paddles inserted at each portage. Then the handles of the paddles are angled outward and tied to the forward thwart or set tight up against the gunnel on each side. The paddles must be

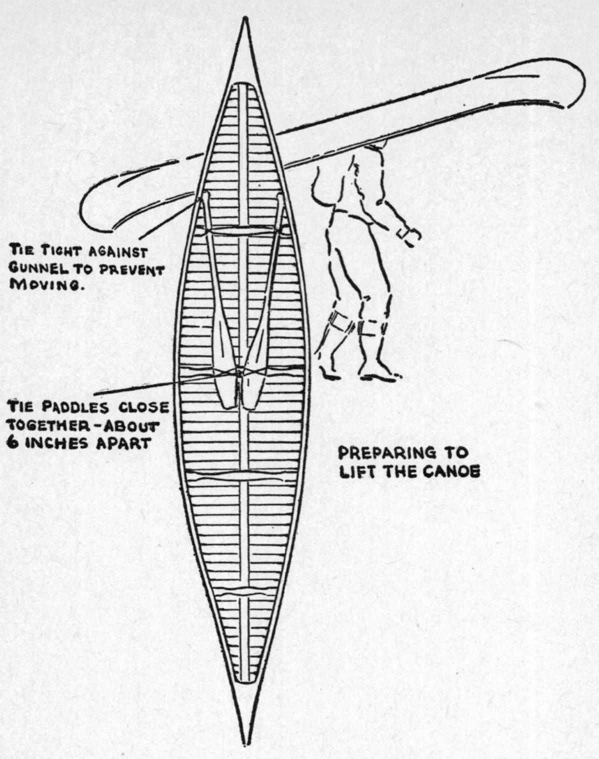



tied firmly so that they won't weave and cut into your neck and shoulders. Some guides use a "tumpline" or "head strap" on the center spreader. I never like this because you have to tie the paddles in anyway. I prefer to carry a Hudson's Bay rucksack with a head strap when carrying a canoe, and take a rest and then carry again. The head strap on the packsack makes a good cushion for the paddle yoke.

If you feel that the canoe is too heavy for you, use a two-man carry as previously described in the chapter on handling the canoe. Your fellow travelers and your guide will respect you for using good sense. Do your share of the carrying, but do not overstrain yourself. Rest regularly, relax, enjoy yourself. That's what you came for. Do your share and a little more, but take care of yourself.

Now back to the portage. Once all gear is ready and the paddle yoke tied in, the sternman takes a light pack, adjusts the head

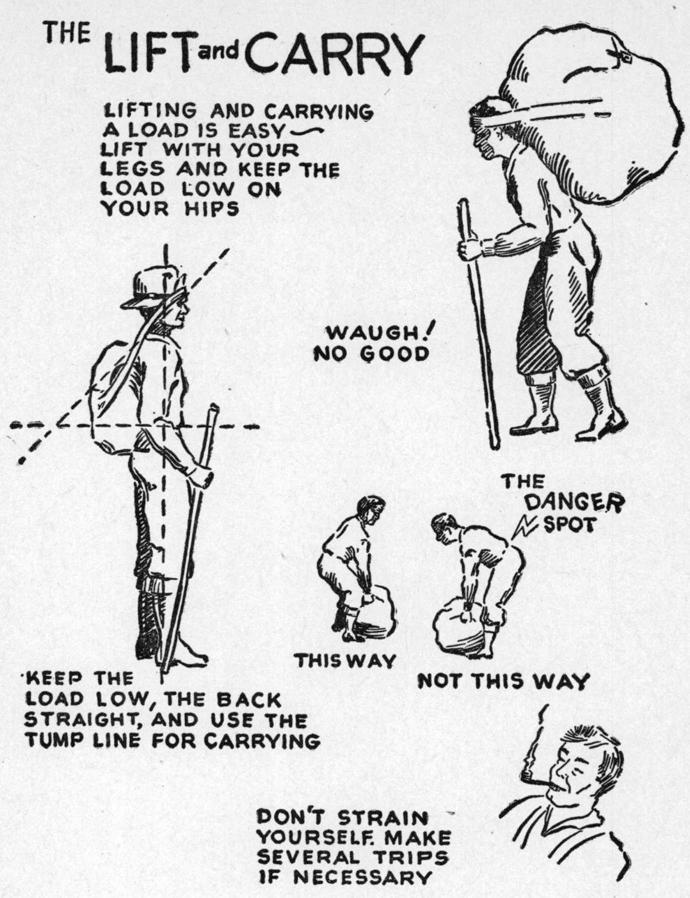



strap, then pulls the canoe up on his knees. He reaches across to the opposite gunnel with his left hand, and with a quick heave, rolls the canoe up onto his shoulders. The bowman stands by to help in adjusting the canoe until it is as comfortable as possible. As soon as all is ready, the bowman loads the rest of the gear on his back and leads the way across the portage trail, advising his companion of any hazards ahead, such as roots, overhead limbs, slippery spots, et cetera. As vision is limited under a canoe, the team should stay together while crossing the portage. It is risky business portaging a canoe alone. I know, as in the canoe country I have had several bad injuries personally and have patched up a great many more among my fellow travelers. Take it slow, easy, careful, and rest regularly. Take time to look around you on the trail. The delights of nature are often best on the portage trails in the canoe country.

The science of carrying is the use of the proper, comfortable equipment, correct suspension and proper balance. After the first few days portaging becomes fun. A word of caution, however. Wear proper footgear to protect your feet and ankles, and never step *on* rocks or logs that you can step *over*. Avoid stepping on roots or slippery clay. Bad falls and injuries can result.

As soon as you are across the portage, load the gear into the canoe, cover it with canvas and tie it down securely. Often it is good to have tea at the end of the portage. Tea is a great help and a morale builder.

When I get a little fat in town, and wonder if I'm getting old, I always head out for a bush trip. I find the satisfaction supreme when I can still take a fifty-pound pack, roll up my canoe and carry over a portage. This is a scale for health and age. When I no longer can carry my own canoe I'll know that my days are numbered, but I hope to have at least another quarter of a century or more before I go to the lands over the great mountain.

*Canoe Gear*

This will be touched on only briefly as it is discussed in detail in my book *Canoe Camping*.

First of all, take everything that you need and nothing that you don't need. I once did guide work for a titled Englishman who insisted on carrying iron tent poles and pegs. I often wonder how they accidentally fell overboard into the lake. The other guide, whose job it was to carry them, never seemed awkward to me. He could ride the logs like a cat, and do spectacular feats of balance in a canoe.

Put everything in a few well-made packsacks, which should have not only shoulder straps but also a comfortable head strap or tumpline of wide, strong, well-oiled leather. All food should be in a canvas or plastic bag, and cameras, film, et cetera, should be in sealed water- and moisture-tight containers. Each canoe should have at least one axe, an extra paddle and fifty feet of one-quarter or three-eighths Manila rope, coiled and fastened to the forward ring by one end, pushed up tight in the bow out of

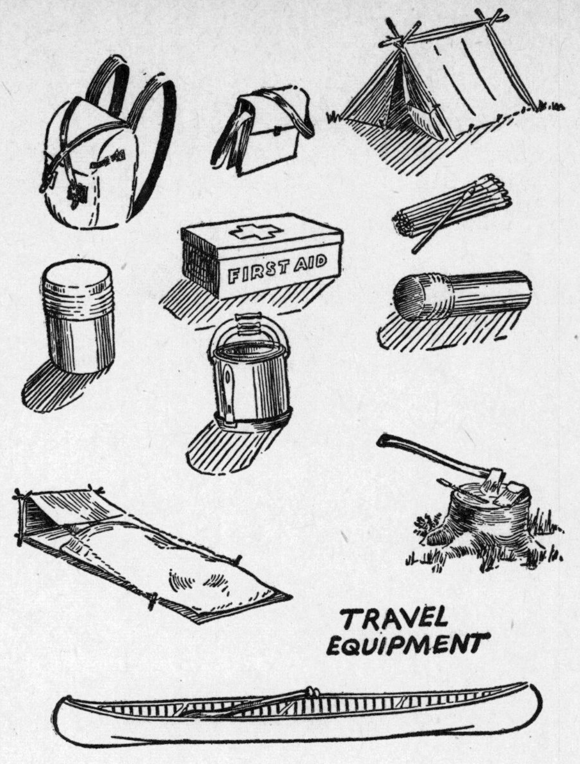



the way. Extra cord or line should always be carried. Fishing rods can be tied under the gunnel. Perishable food should be placed high up in the packsack. The first-aid kit, cameras and fishing gear should be placed on top where they can be reached easily without taking the pack out of the canoe.

Try to have everything loaded into not more than two packs with perhaps a bedroll extra, so that portages can be made in one trip. Take extra canvas for covering your load as well as a half pup tent and a rope to tie it down. Have your poncho ready in case of rain, and a jacket which can be slipped on when you land, especially if the weather is chilly. The latter can also double as a comfortable kneepad.

Proper canoe gear and plenty of food is important to the success of your trip. Preparation of gear and equipment can give you many pleasant months in advance of your trip. Good gear means good canoeing.

*chapter 9*

# Canoe Safety and Repair

The canoe is one of the safest crafts afloat. The canvas-covered or the wooden canoe, if upset, acts as an excellent life preserver. If you have a metal canoe be sure that the air tanks displace enough to float the canoe plus another fifty pounds. Although canoemen seldom upset, there is always that possibility; consequently, when you buy a canoe be sure to test its buoyancy. One of the best ways to test it is to upset it. Then right it, and while it is full of water climb or rather swim in, slide your feet under the gunnels and slowly rise up to a sitting position amidships. If you can sit upright on the bottom of a canoe filled with water, with your shoulders out of the water, and it does not sink, then you have enough buoyancy for safety.

*Getting Out of and Into a Canoe in Deep Water*

SINGLE OVERBOARD IN DEEP WATER     When one man is in a canoe in deep water and wants to take a swim, or for any other reason wants to go overboard, he walks amidship, grasps both gunnels—arms straight, head down, feet center and together— and gets up on his toes. With one motion he springs upward and

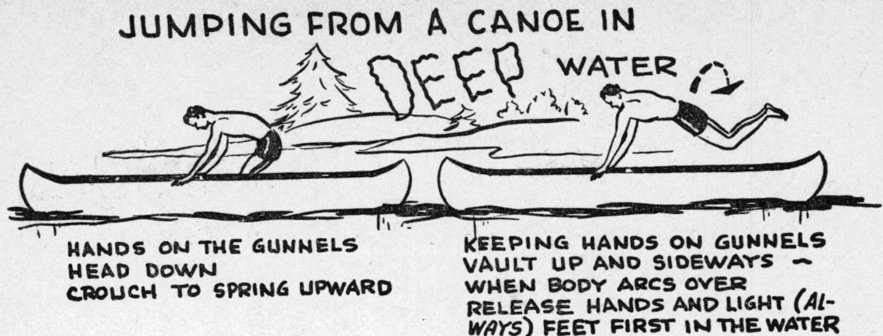



vaults sideways with a half-twist landing, both feet together, in the water facing the side of the canoe. His far hand slides across, and grasping the near gunnel, holds on to the canoe. A word of caution here! It is important to hold on to the canoe, especially if you are on a big body of water. It is a good idea to hold the painter (front rope) in your hand when you jump overboard to insure not being stranded.

SINGLE GETTING ABOARD FROM DEEP WATER    In getting aboard a canoe from deep water, walk your hands along the gunnels until you are just behind the front seat or thwart. Here the canoe is narrow enough to permit you to reach across and grasp the far gunnel with one hand, while the other holds the near gunnel.

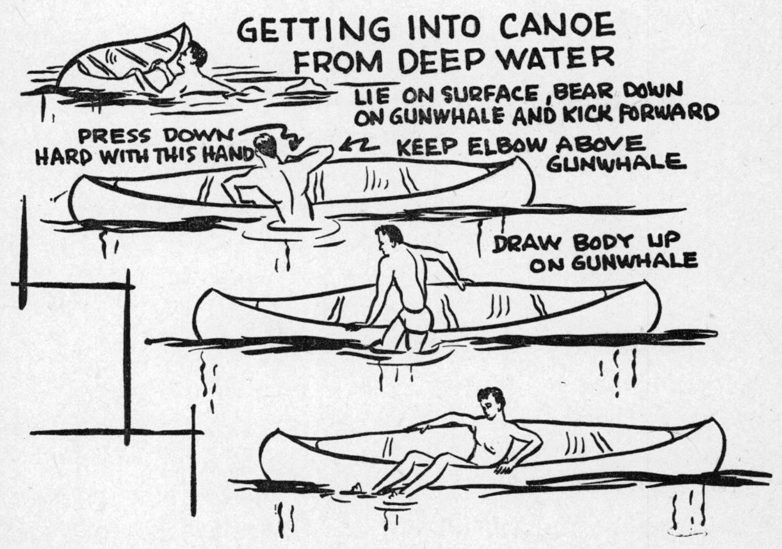

Take a good hold, tilt the canoe slightly toward you, kick with your feet and at the same time push up with your near hand. Slide across the canoe on your stomach, twist facing the stern and sit down quickly in the bottom. This is all done in one continuous motion and should be practiced by everyone who intends to paddle a canoe.

DOUBLE GETTING OVERBOARD IN DEEP WATER    Two men go overboard in the same fashion as singles, one from each end of the canoe. It is best done for one man to steady the canoe by keeling his paddle, while the other vaults over. Then the first man can steady the canoe by holding the gunnel while the second vaults overboard. To accomplish this simultaneously, one man should go over on the port side while the other goes over the starboard side. This takes teamwork and split-second timing. It can be a lot of fun.

TWO MEN GETTING ABOARD IN DEEP WATER    It is simpler for two men to get aboard a canoe in deep water than it is to do it singly. One man holds the opposite gunnel, steadying the canoe, while the other climbs aboard in the same way as described for singles. Then the man aboard keels his paddle, steadying the canoe, while the one in the water comes aboard in the same fashion. The ability to get in and out of a canoe is important to safety in canoeing. It creates a better understanding of the craft and develops confidence.

## Turnover in a Canoe

It is often desirable to turn a canoe over and fill with water to wash it, to look at the bottom, and test its buoyancy. First of all, let us emphasize a general rule for canoeing safety. Never leave rope, string or anything else near the front or back seat or thwart that might catch the feet in case of a turnover, which is always a possibility. You paddle down on your knees with your feet back under the seat or thwart. Keep the area clear of duffel and packstraps. I once had a friend who almost drowned in the Button-Hook rapids by getting his feet caught in a packstrap on the duffel behind him. He was a football player of considerable fame, but if we hadn't reached him in time his career would have ended right there. His canoe had been broken across the middle, and had folded around a rock in the middle of the rapids with him inside. He tried to bail out, but his feet got caught, and if it hadn't been for the wonderful skill and tremendous strength of my old French friend, Oscar Boyer, there would have been a tragedy that day.

A canoe is best turned over by vaulting into the water and pressing down on one gunnel until the canoe fills. A more spectacular way is to get amidships, place your feet on one gunnel, your hand on the other, and when balanced move your backside "jackknife" fashion. The canoe will then tip, fill and turn completely over. This is great fun. You can also stand up on the gunnels amidship and rock back and forth until the canoe dips far enough to fill with water. This usually ends with a complete turnover and a few bruises with barked shins. It is still fun to practice, but be sure you are in deep water.

### Canoe Safety in Case of an Upset

The first rule in case of an upset, especially on big water or in a stream, is to stay with the canoe and get it ashore. The canoe is a good life preserver and can hold you up indefinitely. I saw Lew Hall and Captain Fred Mills, of the National Health and Safety Department of the National Council of Boy Scouts of America, keep eight people afloat in the water by floating motionless, holding for extra support to the sides of the water-filled canoe. It could have held even more. When the canoe is turned bottom side up, the captured air makes is very buoyant.

### Getting Ashore in a Filled Canoe

In case your paddles are lost in an upset and shore is not far away, get into the filled canoe, sit down, leaning back on the center spreader, and use your hands for paddles. In case you have a paddle or can retrieve one, use it, but don't try to hurry. Either way you can get your canoe to shore where it can be emptied. This can be accomplished with either one or two men aboard. You must paddle slowly or the canoe will submerge.

# GETTING INTO A SWAMPED CANOE

### Emptying a Canoe in Deep Water

One should practice emptying a canoe in deep water. Once it has been righted full of water, go to the stern, turn the bow into the wind, and then, holding to the stern wedge, begin to kick, preferably a heavy flutter kick like that used in the crawl stroke. One arm can be used to paddle until the canoe gathers speed. Then kick furiously, and begin to bear down on the stern until the bow raises well up out of the water like an aquaplane. With a final mighty forward kick, the water streams out of the canoe by tilting up the bow and using the forward inertia of the power applied at the depressed stern. Suddenly release the stern, reach a hand under the end of the canoe, and heave up. You will find from one third to one half of the water out of the canoe. Rest, and repeat two or three times until you can get no more out. Then go alongside, just in front or behind the center thwart, and press the canoe down until the gunnel is three or four inches from the water. While holding the gunnel down with the right hand cupped, reach inside the canoe and bail by splashing the water out. I have done this even with the duffel tied in the canoe, but it is better to pull that out, which will float, and pick it up later. If you are near shore with duffel tied in, swim the canoe to shore, unload and empty water out on shore. Don't try to pull a canoe full of water ashore. You run a good chance of wrecking it. Once adjacent to the shore, unload the duffel, put it on the shore, and then roll the canoe bottom up, edge up just enough to let air under. Shove the tip of the canoe up onshore by riding down on the stern. Turn the canoe on its side, lift gently high up out of the water, let it drain, then flop it over right side up and let it dry thoroughly.

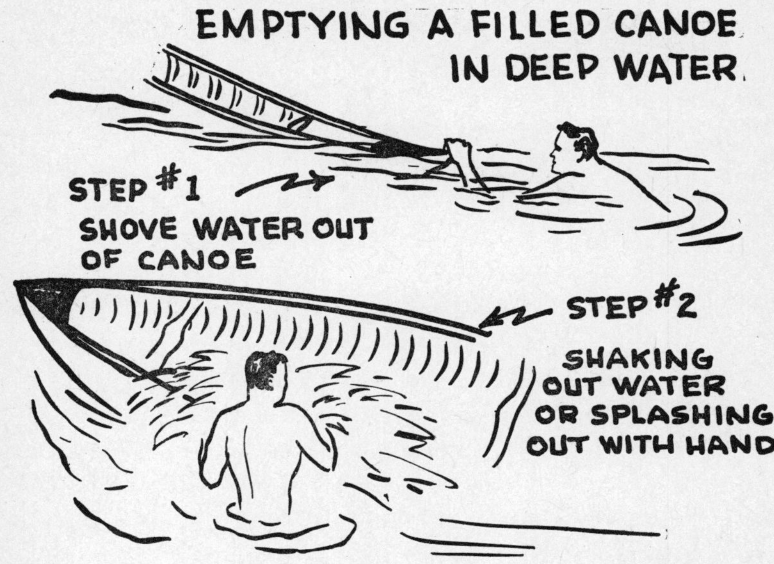


*Shaking the Water Out of a Canoe*

One very spectacular but difficult way of emptying a water-filled canoe is to shake the water out. This takes strength, good water-treading ability and practice. Get amidships and start rocking up and down on the gunnel. Start slowly. The water will slosh back and forth and begin to spill out over the gunnels. Increase the speed of the rocking, and as the canoe stands higher on edge, start shoving outward from you each time. This method, like the other described, has a tendency to shove the canoe out from under the water by inertia. The difference is that in the first method you shove the canoe from the end, and in shaking the water out you shove the canoe out broadside. The round side, being pushed outward, planes upward, helping to spill the water out. I have seen all but a few quarts of water "shaken out" of a filled canoe in less than sixty seconds. If you want to practice, begin by standing waist deep in shallow water with your feet on the bottom. Get the knack of it, then move out into deep water.

Before leaving the subject of the filled canoe, let me point out that the canoe should be washed out and all sand and dirt removed every day during a trip. This is a must, as sand under the feet can grind away the protecting varnish, causing the thin planking to break or rot through. Wash the canoe, scrub it out with a broom or a handful of green twigs and lay it up on shore to dry thoroughly. A canoe is an efficient, faithful friend. Take good care of it and it will serve you well.

## Gunnel Jumping and Playing With a Canoe

A lot of people frown on playing around with an empty canoe, but I personally believe that stunt practicing, especially with younger people, can teach a great deal about balance and about handling a canoe. One of the favorite sports is gunnel jumping. This is done by standing in an empty canoe just in front of the stern seat, facing forward, or just behind the front seat facing the stern. Reach down, grasp the gunnels, then step one foot at a time up on the gunnel. Carefully stand erect and balance the canoe. Toe in, bending the knees slightly, and begin to bob the canoe up and down. Each time you pump your weight up and down, the canoe will move forward a little. A great camp sport is to line up several canoes and have a gunnel-jumping race. It develops balance and skill.

## Canoe Burling

This is a report requiring skill, and as in a log-rolling or burling contest, the object is to take the canoe into deep water and stand up on the gunnels, the two contestants facing each other. At the starting signal, by wobbling gunnels, jumping and shaking, one opponent tries to throw the other off balance into the water without upsetting the canoe. At no time after the starting signal can the canoe be touched by the hands. This contest is inclined to be a little rough, but it is a great test of skill.

## Canoe Tilting and Wrestling

The contestants stand in front of the canoe, each with a ten-foot pole padded on one end. The stern paddler drives his canoe past his opponent, trying to knock him off into the water. The opponent must joust at his adversary only and not at the canoe. This is rough but great sport, and I have seen women do as good a job as men.

## Other Canoe Contests and Sports

In the colorful northern guide meets the above-mentioned sports are used. Besides these, the canoe races are thrilling. Packing contests, portaging races (rough and dangerous) and axe and saw contests, lifting contests and free-for-all wrestling are also used. In the old days dog fights were held, but are now banned. These sports, all traditional in the canoe country, are primarily contests of skill and strength. I personally believe in them, for I believe that safety is best learned through knowledge and skill.

## First Aid

Should an accident occur in the woods where there are no roads, it may be necessary to transport the injured person. In this case the canoe makes an excellent bed and stretcher. When you come to a portage, make four shoulder slings and tie them on each side of the front and back thwarts. At a signal, four people lift and carry. Do not walk in step. Clear the trail wide first. Rest regularly. I know this method well, as I was brought out with a broken hip in 1930 and a broken back in 1946. When you arrive at the railroad tracks, load the patient aboard the baggage coach in the canoe until he can be removed to an ambulance. If need be, the thwarts can be removed to keep from bending him. If you come out at a road, the patient can be hauled in a truck.

In case of injury or unconsciousness in the water, turn the canoe bottom side up and roll the patient on top to be towed ashore. The captured air underneath will buoy him up. In fact, it is best to let some of the air out, as it helps in stabilizing the canoe. You have to balance the upturned canoe carefully or it will roll over.

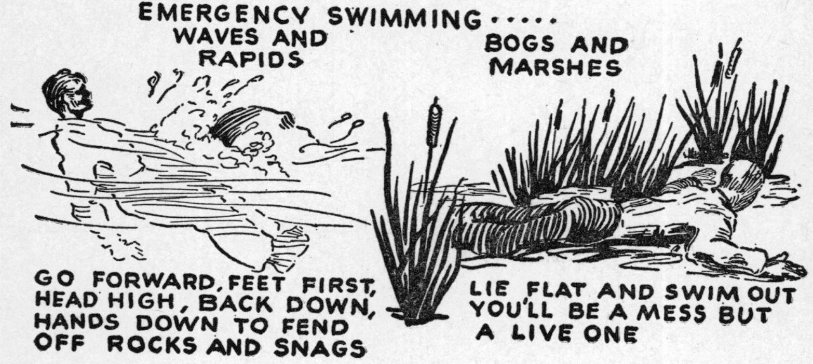


## Canoe Rescue

In case you are alone when your canoe upsets, get the water out as previously described. But if there is another canoe, come alongside immediately, and transfer the duffel and gear to it. When your canoe is empty, turn it at right angles to the rescuing canoe, and with the bow amidships turn bottom side up. One man in the water should go to the opposite side of the rescuing canoe and hold the gunnels for stability, while the filled canoe is drawn bottom side up over the middle of and at right angles to the rescuing canoe. When the overturned canoe is completely out of water, allow it to balance up and drain for a few minutes. Then turn it right side up and slide it back into the water. The man in the water should let go of the gunnels, come around and climb aboard his own canoe, while the rescuing canoe is held steady. All canoemen should know these rescues, as there are many occasions for their use.

One time my friend, Floyd Carpenter, and I pulled a couple out of the Ohio River right opposite downtown Louisville, Kentucky. They had tried very foolishly to ride the wake of boiling water behind a stern-wheeler steamboat. They stood a good chance of being sucked down by the terrific rolling drag. Luckily they had enough sense to hold on to the canoe. We reached them, righted their canoe, got them aboard and they paddled away to shore. Later we found that we didn't know their names nor they ours. We never saw them again.

*Canoe Repair Kit*

It is, of course, the better part of wisdom to avoid any damage to your canoe. But since accidents do happen, a small canoe

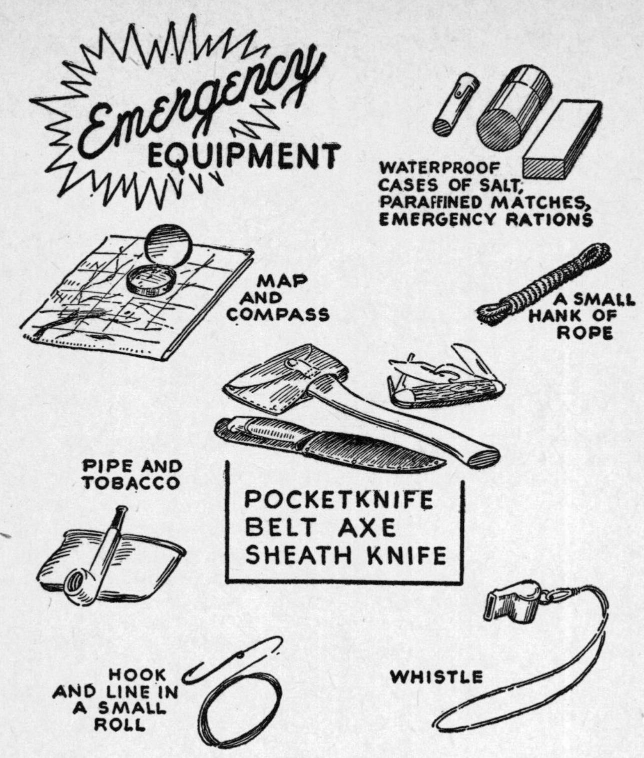


repair kit is a must. It should be packed carefully in a plastic waterproof bag or a compression-top tin can and should contain:

A yard square of 30 Z. duck (often called Egyptian silk)
A roll of brass, copper, or soft iron wire
Brass brads of various sizes
A few brass screws
A small collapsible screw driver
A package of marine glue
A package of one-edged razor blades
A small bottle of shellac or varnish and a brush
A small putty knife
A few yards of fish line
A small pair of long-nose pliers
An awl (sewing awl if possible)
A few common brass pins and safety pins
A few small pieces of emery cloth

These should be packed carefully in a waterproof container and should be fastened tightly into the rear end of the canoe under the wedge.

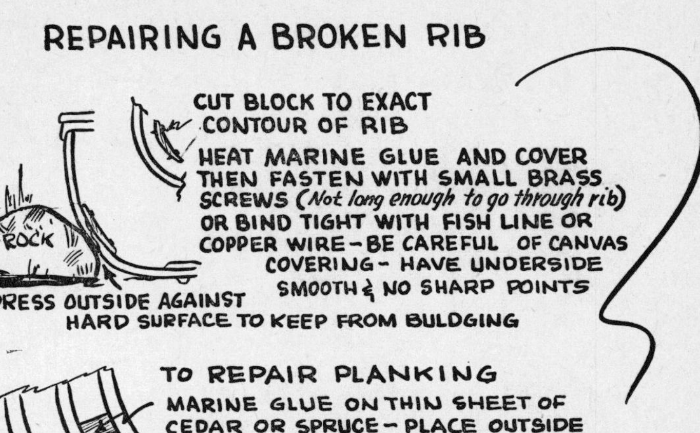


*Canoe Repair*

Take constant care of abrasions and scratches. Dry the damaged places thoroughly. If the cuts pierce the filler, apply some white lead, allow time for drying, then sand lightly and cover with a little waterproof marine glue. Allow the glue to dry, then coat with varnish or shellac.

If the fabric is broken, dry clean thoroughly, apply marine glue and cover with a piece of Egyptian silk, or canvas cloth. If you do not have these materials, birchbark, even brown craft paper or plastic film will work temporarily. Brush on more marine glue, dry thoroughly, then shellac or varnish.

For broken ribs make a section of an over-rib and turn the canoe over. While one person pushes in on the injured rib, the other brads it in and fastens in a few screws. Be sure that the splice is thick enough to prevent brads and screws from going clear through.

Broken gunnels can be braced and spliced in the same manner as a rib and carefully wrapped with copper wire. A broken thwart can also be treated in this way.

# REPAIRING A BROKEN PADDLE

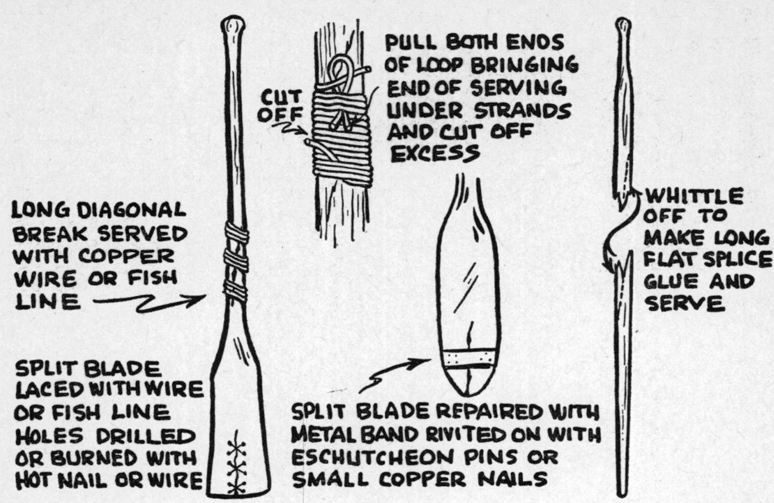


## Paddle Repair

A broken shaft can be splinted and carefully wrapped with soft iron, copper or brass wire. Be sure the wire ends are pulled under so there will be no points on the surface to cut your hands. A split blade can be sewed together with cross-stitching of wire. Drill a series of small holes on each side of the split and sew the wire through. Fasten the ends securely by twisting with pliers and driving the turned end back into the wood.

## Summary

In closing this chapter, let me state that the canoe is one of the most stable and safe crafts of its size afloat. Handle it carefully, especially on land, keep it clean and in constant repair. Explore its possibilities, get in and out of it, turn it over, shake the water out and practice rescues. Understand it as a first-aid transport for the injured and as a vehicle for fun and sport. The canoe is one of the simple, inexpensive pleasures available to everyone. More and more people discover this every year, and they find a whole new world of interest and travel. You too can become a canoe enthusiast and know the lure of the lakes, streams and waterways of our land and others.

*chapter* **10**

# Afterglow

We sat by the fire of willow branches and chunks of dwarfed spruce augmented by a pile of dried caribou dung. An early quarter-moon hung red in the October sky, and the first reaching fingers of the northern lights began to play their silent symphony up a blue-black sky perforated by thousands of brilliant stars. Away up to the horizon swept the edge of the tundra land that had changed from greens to the golden rolling prairie of early autumn. Tea steamed in the battered old graniteware pot that had served for making both coffee and tea until the coffee ran out a month or two earlier. Joe Sotherland, an Eskimo, rolled out two bundles from the glowing coals and opened them up. They exuded the aroma of baked char (a troutlike fish caught in the subarctic) stuffed with a slice of bacon and flavored and spiced with salt and cracked peppercorn. A piece of bannock was taken from the frying pan used as a reflector oven. All ate silently, and I watched the fading moonlight and increasing northern lights play on the long stretch of black water in the lake for miles up to the horizon. Light glinted on the upturned bottoms of our faithful canoes that had carried us over a thousand miles in the past months.

High in the night came a faint sound like that of hounds or the squeak of the axles of a dead-ax wagon in need of grease. It increased in volume until the sky resonated with the bugle sounds of thousands of geese flying like a compass point to the south over phantom roads in the sky known only to them. The chorus finally faded, but it left the land awake around us. There was the sudden gust of a breeze that faded as quickly as it came. My half-Cree pardner said the first words in a deep quiet voice just above a whisper that reflected the deep undertone of the land for ages long before the black robes came: "The great Buda (bird raven of legend) has flown by us and the Winabashoo has spoken storm talk on the night wind."

Far down the lake a cow moose called across the waters and was answered in the distant hills by the deep rumbling of a bull moose. Far away an old dog wolf gave a long cry that was picked up by others as they sang to the hunter's moon, then it stopped as though a button had been pushed. The silence crowded in, and the long slurring cry of a fox went along the bottom of the ridge a mile away to scare the arctic hares so they would run up the ridge to where mama fox was waiting. A muffled squeaking cry followed and, after a pause, a brief yapping bark told us that mama fox was calling papa fox to dinner. "Toquees," the mouse, rustled the leaves and came out to look at us with large liquid eyes.

The spell was broken and we knew that the time had come to say good-by to all of this. We would have to leave our two Eskimos to face the northern winter while we raced south up great rivers and over lakes to the Canadian National Railway tracks where I would go on alone into the noisy labyrinth of civilization.

The handle of the Great Bear in the sky showed that it was near midnight and time to leave. Gear had been stripped down to a minimum and the frost crackled as we walked to the canoes. The season of the winds was soon to roar down out of the north and we would paddle at night on the big lakes to avoid the rough waters. Ice crackled as we slid the canoes into the lake and stowed a couple of well-worn packs and a bedroll aboard and tied them down. Out across the lake, ghost wisps of mist hung low over the surface. The moon had now gone down and the northern lights flickered and blazed, making an eerie scene in the phosphorescent mist.

We had left our extras and instruments to Joe's safekeeping and had delayed our departure until the signs told us that we must race King Winter before he sealed our water highway for many months with a steely grip of ice. Joe loaded his canoe, we shook hands and paddled out a little way into the lake together and then said good-by again. We turned south and they north, and in a moment they were swallowed up by the mist, and the swish of our paddles drove our faithful canoe toward home. After ten minutes of paddling, from away down the lake came the long cry of the loon, which we recognized as Joe, and I answered with a long cry of the timber wolf—a final farewell.

We pulled on in deep thought and dreams of the wonderful days together in our faithful canoes. We were traveling in the age-old way in these wonderful craft over wild highways that could be traversed in no other way in the summer season.

The privilege of these experiences has been so great that friends urged me to share their secrets in this book so that you too can sit by little fires in faraway places with your faithful canoe. Try canoeing as a thrilling recreation and sport and maybe the great Buda (bird) will fly by your fire at night and fan it with his wings and the Winabashoo on the night wind will whisper to you of faraway places.

MAY THE END BE THE
BEGINNING

# Index